MY CORNWALL

EDITED

BY

MICHAEL WILLIAMS

BOSSINEY BOOKS

First published in 1973
by Bossiney Books
St Teath, Bodmin, Cornwall
Typeset and printed in Great Britain by
Penwell Ltd, Parkwood, Callington,
Cornwall

ISBN 0 906456 28 2

MY CORNWALL

* * *

INTRODUCTION

Cornwall is different things to different people. Her attractions are subtle and several-sided.

Painters, since Thomas Rowlandson towards the end of the 18th century, have found inspiration here. Some have stayed for a while, enjoyed a Cornish period and gone again ; others have stayed a lifetime. The same is true of writers. They too have felt the lure ; some driven by hard economic necessity in that they have found a cheaper way of living ; others hailed by some magical, compelling voice.

Much has been written and painted and created here — probably more than anywhere outside London.

But why Cornwall ?

The question is inevitable, fascinating, recurring and almost certainly unanswerable.

It is not as simple as defining the ingredients of a real Cornish pasty. I am by no means certain you would get 100% agreement among native housewives on those basic gastronomic facts ! Perhaps there is no single crystal-clear explanation about Cornwall's magnetism. Maybe Denys Val Baker got somewhere near the truth when he reflected : " It is a mixture of material and mystical, facts and fantasies, all equally important."

And it is deeper and wider than sheer creativity in the arts. Traditional industries have waned, almost disappeared. Take a look at those ivy-coated skeletons of the engine houses with their round brick chimneys in the old mining country : symbols of a Cornish industry which has nearly vanished. The noise of labour — with one or two exceptions — died long ago. Fishing and farming now need fewer hands. Tourism has become the golden goose. Year after year, more and more people come to Cornwall : a recharging of human batteries. Many make it an annual pilgrimage ; a percentage even uproot and finally retire in the Westcountry, but some taste Cornwall once and never come again.

Identity too is difficult, for Cornwall is a kingdom, not a county. Mosaic might be a better word. With a language and a heritage of her own, Cornwall defies neat easy classification. She is no gentle shire belonging to Saxon England. No true Cornishman would call her English. There is a rich diversity about these lands and seascapes. Study our south and north coasts, one soft, the other harsh. Who would connect the two ? Who would give them a common adjective other than Cornish ?

You walk down a lane and round a corner, and you find yourself in another world. You climb the shoulder of a valley and meet a stranger.

Perhaps appropriately I am writing these lines on the last day of an old year, appropriately because divisions in Cornwall — at times — seem thin ; doors open and close quietly, almost inaudibly ; even the calendar itself can look ridiculous when say November borrows a morning from the month of May or an August afternoon assumes a near Judgment Day quality with clouds making a low ceiling in an inky sky.

Said Thomas Burke of Tintagel : " What it has to give must be received individually . . " Burke didn't realize it, but he was speaking of all Cornwall : north, south, east and west.

My Cornwall is an apt title because for many of us Cornwall is a very personal and precious place. But a sentence of warning: this is no guide book — that was not our intention — moreover we are merely portraying eleven Cornwalls. Nobody knows — or will ever know — how many there are. However I hope and believe these pages will add something significant to the Cornish library : eleven writers, living and writing in the county, writing about their Cornwall. As a painter alters our vision, so a writer with words can open our eyes and deepen our understanding.

Here then are eleven intensely personal interpretations.

M.W.

Bossiney House Hotel
Tintagel

Daphne du Maurier

The Claw of Cornwall

Cornwall projects from the body of England much as Italy falls from the land mass of central Europe. The two peninsulas, so dissimilar in size, are curiously alike in shape ; both long, narrow, terminating in a pincer movement — the claw of Cornwall probing the grey Atlantic, while Italy's high-heeled boot, more delicately formed, treads the Ionian Sea. Resemblance goes further, for each has a river in the north, spanning its breadth and flowing eastward : the Italian Po rising in Monte Viso near the French frontier and coursing to the Adriatic, the Cornish Tamar, its source close to the Devon border, making a natural boundary between Cornwall and Devon for fifty-seven and a half miles before it enters the English Channel.

The analogy might be pushed to its limit, comparing Italy's vertebrae, the central Apennines, with Cornwall's backbone, that high hinterland running from north to south, comprising Bodmin moor, the uplands of St. Breock and the startling perimeter of the china-clay district dominating Hensbarrow downs, where the white soil heaps thrust skyward, a mountain range in miniature. This said, the parallels can be dismissed, the map of Europe folded and Italy, birthplace of the Roman Empire, cradle of the Renaissance, centre of art and learning throughout the centuries, culminating today in a new brilliance of industrial achievement and design, be left to her immortality.

3

Cornwall, little known, of small significance, remains the tail of England, still aloof and rather splendidly detached from the activity across Tamar hailed as progress ; yet aware, despite her seeming isolation, that in those distant ages when Britons beyond the river were tilling the soil and grazing cattle, the first settlers near the Land's End were already streaming tin, trading their mineral wealth with successive immigrants from Iberia and the Mediterranean lands to the east, and so glimpsing a civilization hitherto unknown, ancient, wondrous, secreting amidst the Cornish soil the golden crescents and the blue beads of Crete.

This is no flight of fancy ; these things have been found in the barrow graves of Cornwall. Who brought them from their places of origin, what venturers from the Aegean and the Mirtoon seas, braving the Atlantic Ocean in ships undaunted by the rugged coasts of Brittany and Ireland, to find haven at long last in Cornwall's river Hayle, cannot be known with certainty. They are said to have been short and dark — but so were the later Celtic immigrants from France. Romantics of the nineteenth century and our own time, seeking an explanation for a black-haired beauty down Camborne way, or a dark-eyed fisherman casting his nets with easy grace from a vessel in Mount's Bay, would insist — and this was believed by the Cornish themselves — that men and women with such foreign looks must be descended from those unfortunate sailors who had been cast away upon the Cornish beaches when the Spanish Armada was defeated in 1588. If so, the Spanish sailors had a genius for begetting, re-producing themselves a thousandfold. It is more logical and exciting, to go back to some 1400 years B.C. and remember earlier dark-eyed seamen, with narrow waists and braided hair, whose brothers back in Knossos, may have leapt the Cretan bull.

There is in the Cornish character, smouldering beneath the surface, ever ready to ignite, a fiery independence, a stubborn pride. How much of this is due to centuries of isolation after the Roman conquest of Britain, when Mediterranean trade no longer found its way to south-western estuaries but went direct from Roman France to the eastern channel ports, and how much to the legacy of those dark-haired invaders with their blue beads and their circlets of gold, heirs of a civilization existing long before Rome was even named, is something the Cornish can argue for themselves. As an outsider, with Breton forebears, I like to think that the two races, facing an Atlantic seaboard blown by identical gales, washed by the same driving mists, share a common ancestry, along with the Irish further west.

Superstition flows in the blood of all three peoples. Rocks and stones, hills and valleys, bear the imprint of men who long ago buried their dead beneath great chambered tombs and worshipped the earth goddess. Nowhere else in England do these symbols of eastern ritual stand, but here in Cornwall the tombs are with us still. Great slabs of granite, weather-pitted, worn, with another mighty slab, tip-tilted, to form a roof ; these were the burial places of priests, perhaps of queens. Set in the high places, amidst scrub and gorse, the treasures they once contained long rifled by barbarians and the bones scattered, they stand as memorials to a forgotten way of life and a once-living cult. Sometimes today the setting is incongruous — a small field, perhaps, with a line of bungalows near by. Yet age has not destroyed their majestic beauty, nor plough and tractor tumbled the foundations. The stones, like the natural granite cast up from the earth by nature, defy the centuries. To stand beside them, whether on the heights of West Penwith, amongst the bracken of Helman Tor or in the little field above St. Cleer, is to become, as it were, an astronaut in time. The present vanishes, centuries dissolve, the mocking course of history with all its triumphs and defeats is blotted out. Here in the lichened stone is the essence of memory itself. Whether it was priest or chieftain, queen or priestess, who lay here once, prepared with solemn rites for the passage to the underworld, belief in immortality was theirs, Man's answer, from the beginning, to the challenge of death.

These, then, were the first tombs of Cornwall ; but scattered throughout the length and breadth of the Peninsula are other stones and other chambers, barrows and trenches, mounds and circles, so that it might be said that death, like the sea, is ever present. There is always a reminder, on some ridge or hillside, half-concealed perhaps by thorn or bracken, that stillness waits.

Later generations, with the guilt engendered by Puritan or Methodist upbringing, thought all standing or leaning stones were persons frozen by the merciless hand of God for dancing on a Sunday. Or so at least they told their children, though perhaps they knew better. For although, in those early days, they might not connect death and burial with the mounds and the old tilted stones in field and furze, they sensed that the place held magic, and whatever dwelt there under a brooding sky should be placated. Instinct, infallible, bade them place a hand upon the mound or stone, and spit. If the stone had a hole in it, like the Mên-an-Tol near Lanyon, the wisest thing to do was to crawl through it nine times against the sun. To crawl against the sun " backened " disease. The isolation that kept Cornwall from the rest of England thus preserved an ancient lore, an intuitive perception of things past.

The underworld that promised immortality held its treasures too, so that Cornishmen, from the beginning, have always dug for wealth. They were, are, tinners, copper-seekers, quarriers, slate-breakers, clay-workers, farmers ; an earthy people with an earthy knowledge, the word earthy used not as a slight but as a salutation.

Those who desire to understand the Cornish, and their country, must use their imagination and travel back in time.

The right way to approach Cornwall is from the sea, sailing from southern Ireland to the Hayle estuary, as the first traders did in those centuries B.C. — and surely with the same shock of surprise and relief, after a stormy passage, with the prevailing sou'westerly wind veering between the quarter and hard astern to find that the inhospitable rock-bound Cornish claw thrusting into the Atlantic in quest of victims has, to the immediate north-west of its scaly hump, a welcome haven. Then, as today, the contrast was profound between the forbidding grandeur of the coast-line about Land's End, with its hinterland of granite tors, and the sudden emergence of St. Ives Bay, an encircling arm protecting the shallows and the yellow sands and the estuary of Hayle ; but then, unlike today, the river, broad and deep, was tidal inland for four miles or more, cutting nearly to Mount's Bay on the south coast. Hayle was a natural refuge, the obvious centre for a trading population who, building trackways beside the river valley, could barter their tin to vessels coming from both the Atlantic and the Channel sea-routes.

The estuary, alas, is now, and has been through the centuries, silting up. A narrow channel, marked with straggling poles to warn the venturing seaman of the ever-encroaching banks of sand, leads to the once flourishing port. Even the yachtsman dares not hazard the passage that long ago offered shelter and opportunity for trade to Bronze Age seamen.

For the watcher today, crouching amidst the sand-dunes and the tufted grass, looking seaward to where the shallows run, imagination can take a riotous course, picturing line upon line of high-prowed flat-bottomed craft, brightly coloured, their sails abeam, entering the river with the flood tide. What cries and oaths, what turbulence of Mediterranean chatter interspersed with Irish, as the traders ran their vessels on the sand or anchored them to swing midstream ; what speedy loading or unloading of cargo between ship and settlement, what feasting, when the work was done, beside a fire of turf and furze ; what interchange of vows, with dance and conquest !

The image fades, and the dreamer, stiff from crouching in the dunes, sees how the sand has, through the centuries, invaded the coastal countryside north of Hayle. Hurricanes, in the long-distant past, whipped up the swirling mass into dense clouds which settled on the land below. Whole farmsteads were over-whelmed and now lie buried, while the waste land known as the towans, a mixture of sand and sea-rush — a stiff-stemmed reedy grass planted in old days by the inhabitants to stay the driving sand — stretches through Phillack and Gwithian parishes until the ground rises into the headland of Godrevy Point. Gales and storms have been ever frequent on both north and south Cornish coasts, bringing havoc and disaster with them and a multitude of wrecks, but a hurricane of sand, destroying homes, was the grim fate of these Gwithian farmers near to Hayle. A winter gale will spend its force, the seas grow calm, the rains cease ; the sand is a more insidious enemy. During one tempestuous winter of the nineteenth century there was a sudden shifting of the sands, and the long-buried farmstead of Upton was exposed to view, roof and walls preserved like a villa in Pompeii. People came from near and far to gaze in wonder. Then the wind and sand rose in unison, and Upton Barton was buried once again.

Beyond Upton, close to where the river Connor empties its rusty waters into the sea — the river known as the Red because of the residue of tin staining the surface and washing the banks from the old mines near the source — there are other ruins beneath the sand, disturbed from time to time by wandering cattle. Here lies the Oratory of St. Gothian, who gave his name to Gwithian parish and was supposedly a martyr. Today there is nothing left but a few scattered stones, the sand about them seeping red. What manner of man it was who prayed here and preached redemption none can say.

Many a pilgrim, staff in hand, afire with early Christian zeal, set foot in Hayle from Wales and Ireland, to be called, in later years, a Cornish saint. Their names are legion. There are more parishes named after founder-saints scattered across the length and breadth of Cornwall than anywhere else in the rest of England. One thing is certain : the saints bore little likeness to later-day parish priests. Some of them were hermits or holy-men, with a knowledge of herbs and remedies for ills, inheritance of an older lore that could be turned to good account, magic interwoven with the sign of the Cross. They lived on rocks and promontories, beside streams or near to the sea's edge, and the prayers they uttered awoke in the converted a memory of incantations in the past.

Others dwelt closer to their flock, and, like the preaching Methodists of our own times and the worker priests of France at the factory bench, won respect from their fellow-men because of skill with hands as well as with tongue, becoming, without deliberate intent, leaders within a group. As to St. Gothian, whose bones may or may not lie beneath the ruined Oratory on the towans, it is good to think of him streaming for tin somewhere near the Connor source, then descending to the bay to offer thanks, his ankles rusty red and caked with the sand, carrying in his hands as an emblem to faith a thunder-axe or pick.

Other saints, like the Welshman Samson, avoided the likely inhospitality of Hayle and reached Cornwall by way of the Camel estuary. For the approach to Cornwall can be made in many ways, dangerously as of old, like seafarer or saint, braving the short seas and the shifting sands of Hayle and Camel, which can only be recommended to the intrepid with a genius for pilotage ; or more leisurely as yachtsman, seeking the broader, safer and more welcoming waters of the Fal and Fowey estuaries, whose seaports, unlike forgotten Hayle, still offer haven

8

to shipping from the world and carry a thriving trade. These estuaries, winding and deeply wooded in their upper reaches, seem a world away from sand-swept Hayle and Camel on the northern coast, though little more than sixteen miles separate Fal from the first and Fowey from the second.

Even the climate is more temperate. Here the rain, no longer driving across high barren ground where the stunted trees are blown backwards by its force, falls in a mizzle. A sluggish indolence pervades. The stranger, coaxing his boat up-river in a sudden windless calm, ignoring the busy harbours, casts anchor with a yawn beside pool or creek, then lolls by the tiller, too idle to row ashore. Peace prevails. The tide ebbs. The gently wooded slopes on either side of him that seemed at first sight to touch the water's edge appear more distant. Mud-banks form beneath them, oozing and soft, or little steep-to beaches of grey slate.

Birds, save for the gulls that piloted him to port, have hitherto been absent. Now they are everywhere. Oyster-catchers — sea-pie to the Cornish — with a quick seeping cry, swoop to the mud-banks in a flash of black and white. The smaller redshank and sanderling scurry to probe the slate. Further up-river, where a dead branch from a fallen tree, strung about with seaweed, overhangs the water, a heron stalks, prinking his way like some grave professor fearing to lose a galosh, then suddenly stands and broods, his wings humped, his head buried in his feathers. Later the tide slackens, the trees darken, the birds are hushed, and there is no sound except the whisper of water past the anchor chain until, if the yachtsman is lucky, he will hear, during the magic moments before true dusk falls, the night-jar call. It is a summons unlike any other, churring, low, strangely compelling, so that on first hearing it you must think of neither bird nor beast but of some forgotten species, a scaly lizard cross-bred with a toad. There is no sweetness here, no nightingale passion, no owl foreboding ; the call is primitive, insistent, with a rhythmic rise and fall, coming not from the wooded slopes but from open ground beyond, where amidst foxglove and gorse the night-jar crouches.

The silence of the upper reaches of Fowey river, and of those of Fal and Helford too, broken today by the chug of diesel and outboard engine, a passing irritant, was less intense in the

9

distant past, when their forking branches were tidal further inland, and ships of depth could discharge cargoes at the ancient river ports, now sleeping villages by the stream's edge. Gweek and Constantine on Helford, Tregony on Fal, Lostwithiel on Fowey, knew maritime greatness as late as the sixteenth century, the channels deep enough for vessels to cast anchor or make fast to the stone quays. Another estuary, now sand-barred and impenetrable, cut inland past Tywardreath to St. Blazey bridge, and if the eye follows the course of the marsh between the hills where the railway now runs it becomes instantly perceptible why King Mark of Cornwall built his fortress on the high ground at Castle Dor, commanding the sea entrances to east and west.

Such, then, was the seafarer's approach to Cornwall in olden times ; but the invader from overland had first to ford the Tamar, and the traveller who does this today in his fast-moving car can become, for a brief moment, a Roman legionary or a Saxon king.

There are some thirteen bridges across the Tamar now, the last being only seven years old, running parallel to Brunel's railway bridge from Plymouth to Saltash. There were none before the Normans conquered England, and the Romans, like the Saxons, would have forded the river high up-stream, close to the river's source, or pushed on beyond the marshy bed to the high ground above, where some four miles only separate Tamar from the sea. Had ingenious diggers in the past made a vast trench linking the Tamar source with the secondary stream that rises near to it and hurtles down to Marsland Mouth, Cornwall would have been an island. Invasion might, for a decade longer, have been held at bay. As it was the enemy rode and conquered finding that the high ground formed a backbone across the narrow breadth of Cornwall.

Today a main road covers the same worn track, bearing the traveller to Camelford, where Saxon Egbert defeated the Cornish at Slaughter Bridge. If, unlike Egbert, he has a peaceful nature and a taste for exploration, he may descend from the car, climb the banks and try to find the Tamar's source. It will take him many hours, plodding in frustration from field to field through splashy marsh, until a trickle of water, splurging from a bog and coursing east, makes him shout " Eureka!" to a companion out of earshot three fields away. He may, or may not, have found the Tamar, but whatever the stream may be triumph is complete, and he knows a conquerer's pride.

2

Ronald Duncan

One Foot in either County

As the boundary of Devon and Cornwall runs through my land, I have one foot in either county. Indeed there is a small half-acre field which I am told is neither, and on which I could seek refuge from arrest were I to commit murder.

Boundaries are marked on the map, but they are merely a convenience of county government, or do they delineate any geographical feature ?

The present tendency in government and culture is towards centralisation and uniformity, and I suppose that within fifty years such local boundaries will be of little but historical interest.

However, today, motoring from Seaton to Lynton you know almost to within a mile when you have crossed the border of Somerset ; and similarly going from Bideford to Plymouth, you know immediately you are in Cornwall. It is not a question of seeing the more spacious parklands of Somerset give way to the pocket-handkerchief fields of Devon, or of noticing the ordered orchards break down to the ancient unpruned trees covered with Old Man's beard. It may be that it is not one particular thing which gives you the feeling that you are now in a different county, but many small details which you do not notice by themselves. It may be that Somerset gates are of a different shape to Devon gates : each county of England has such idiosyncrasies.

The Cornish road is smooth compared to the Devon corrugated switchbacks; no sign post is necessary to mark the boundary between Devon and Cornwall: the bump on the tarmac is sufficient.

I am often asked why I live away from London, where it is generally assumed I should reside; I have never been able to give a satisfactory answer.

I could have settled anywhere. As it is, I have spent a considerable part of my life living on the North Cornwall and Devon coast. I first came to spend a holiday here when I was about four years old, and it may well be that the childish impression I received then determined my choice years later.

I recollect now that on the last day of term at school we were always given a large sheet of cartridge paper and told we could draw whatever we wished. I cannot even draw square, but I do remember that on these occasions I would always try and reproduce the vivid impression I had in my mind of the Marsland Valley. My efforts were crude: I would merely draw a capital V with a bar across it. When asked what this single letter was supposed to indicate, I would reply: it is Marsland Valley; the sides are the hills, the cross-piece is the sea. To me, the picture seemed quite adequate.

The land from Hartland down to Bude is broken by innumerable valleys like Marsland. They are mostly uninhabited, and contain an old derelict water mill. The sheds of land are about two miles long, and are generally flanked by self-sown woods of scrub oak, where all the trees have trunks like cork-screws, and the branches are shorn from the west with each twig pointing away from the cruel wind. As the valley approaches the sea, the woods give way to gorse, ling and the principal crop of bracken. And even today I can often see a motionless buzzard hovering over the great cliffs, as I watch the gulls returning from the ploughland, scissoring the air out to sea.

These valleys are too silent to be anything but sinister, and I suppose too uncared-for to be really beautiful. For dereliction always carries with it an atmosphere of futility and despair. To look at these broken-down old water-mills, where the wheel has long since ceased to turn and lies with its rim all rusted and its buckets broken ; where the stable which used to house the donkeys that carried corn now holds nothing but a few bits and pieces of driftwood ; and where ivy throttles the old cob wall, is to see too vivid an image of human impotence against time and nature for the picture to be pleasant, the conclusion to be comfortable.

Yet it was in such a derelict water-mill that I chose to settle. Why ? It did not attract me in the way that parkland satisfies me with its ordered elegance and suggestion of social, almost emotional, security. Perhaps it did not attract me at all, but challenged me ; and at twenty, one is not sufficiently wise to ignore such challenges. Consequently I spent the next few years trying to reclaim this old mill until the wheel turned again, giving the house electricity ; and yet immediately this was done, I moved from there to a farm overlooking the valley, where I still live.

To move from one house to another is to do more than change one's address. We think it is merely a matter of shifting our furniture, buying new curtains, finding new tradesmen. Such tedious business accomplished, we unpack our books and assume quite confidently that our personality will soon impose itself on our new surroundings, and that we shall then feel quite at home again ; and everything will be as before. That is where we make a big mistake: it is not we who change a house but, more often, the house which changes us. Anyhow, that has been my experience.

As I say, I had had my eye on this old water-mill for years. The beach was only two hundred yards from the mill. Wild sage and thyme made the cliffs smell like Harris tweed. The land had been entirely abandoned to rabbits ; the small trout stream was leased by a heron, and poised buzzards overlorded all.

I do not know why I had wanted to live in this place. Perhaps I mistook its solitude would mean serenity. At any rate, as soon as I heard that the Mill was vacant, I went down the steep cart track to look over the place. The old miller, who had recently moved to a farm at the top of the hill, now trundled along beside me. I noticed his legs were bandy, like two barrel staves ; and that his enormous shoulders were bent as from a life in carrying great weights — but, as he was a miller, this did not surprise me.

The cottage looked rather like a drunken charwoman, for its thatch had slipped over its eaves ; the untidy ivy hung as wisps over its blowsy walls.

"It's got great character, this house has," said the miller, trying to impress me. He was right ; this cottage had character, but of what kind was another matter. At that moment I suspected that any references his old char might produce would be forged in her own untidy hand.

"And it's old as the hills themselves," the miller added in the vague hope that its vice might have decreased with its age.

We went inside. There were only three rooms. And, if one excluded the large open fire-place from the sitting room, then one would say there were only two.

The cottage was unfurnished but full: full of clutter. My wife and I had to stand on each other's feet for the floor was covered with the queerest assortment of rubbish that I had ever seen. Bits of cork, coils of rope, slabs of grease, lumps of brass and planks of every length. In one bedroom I observed five unhung doors lying in a pile on a bed.

"I'll clear this stuff out," the miller offered, trying to make a deal.

"What about water ?" I asked him.

"There's a well."

"A lavatory ?"

"There's a bucket."

"You only need some nails and you could be a fakir," my wife suggested to me.

"With inconveniences like these," I retorted, pointing to the pump without a handle, "none of our friends will ever visit us. This is just the place we're looking for."

I was, at that time, trying to write a play. I was fleeing from London distractions. And, mistaking discomfort for simplicity, I bought the cottage there and then.

15

"What are we going to do about furniture?" my incredibly tolerant wife asked.

The miller offered to sell us a single bed, a card-table and a rocking-chair.

"As for the rest, you'll soon pick up that," he said with a tired sort of recognition which I didn't notice at the time.

Having removed his pile of doors from the bed, he puffed his way up the hill again.

My wife surveyed her home.

"It won't take you long to dust it," I consoled her, "once he's cleaned this stuff out." Then I took my turn in our only chair as she went to explore the cupboards.

"This is just the place to write in," I mused. And, as a gesture, I began, absent-mindedly to sharpen a pencil . . . And that was as near as I got to my play; for, at that moment, there was a cry of excited delight coming from the depths of the cupboard underneath the stairs . . . My wife had found an old rusty kettle, two cups and a knife.

"If you were to stop wasting your time, sharpening a pencil," she said as she emerged, covered in cobwebs, "and were to go and find some firewood, we could boil this kettle and have some tea."

"If we had any tea," I replied, bluntly puncturing her domestic fantasy.

"Anyhow, if you get some firewood, we could sit by the fire, or, at least, one of us could."

I put the pencil down. It was a full four years before I picked it up again.

I went outside and immediately began tugging at the gorse roots. Either they were strong or I was weak. When we parted, I was the more dishevelled. Feeling discouraged, I wandered aimlessly down the donkey path to the beach. The tide was just on the turn. A faint evening wind blew from the land, turning the backs of the waves as though they were the leaves of a book. For a few moments I stood watching, almost mesmerised by the monotonous sound of the waves as they broke on the indifferent beach. Then, quite suddenly, I saw something more interesting, something bobbing up and down about three waves out from the shore. For a moment I thought it was a seal, for I'd often watched them along this coast on a calm day. Then the surf seemed to roll itself into one great wave which flung the object toward me. It was a small wooden keg. I rolled it out of the sea, far too excited to notice that I was by now almost soaked to the skin. Then, with hands as clumsy as a crab, I began to claw at the lid. I could tell by its weight that it was full — but of what ? In desperation, I looked for a sharp pebble, and with it bashed a hole in the lid. I smelt. I stuck my finger in. I sucked. It was fresh butter. About fifty pounds of it. Like a prospector who had at last found gold by tripping over a mine, breaking his nose on a nugget, I began to giggle hysterically. Then, finding the strength I did not know I possessed. I carried the keg back to the cottage.

" Butter from the beach," I announced, placing it before my wife, as though that now completed her home.

She dug her finger in. " It's perfect ! " she said. " What a pity we haven't got any bread . . . "

That's how it began ; and, for the next seven years, the tide never turned but I was there to meet it. And the tide turns twice a day. The fascination of finding something for nothing now dominated me. Often I would wake up at four o'clock in the morning, hearing the wind moaning over the cottage. For a few seconds I would lie still, wondering what might be cast up on the rocks. Perhaps another keg ? This time, some tea ? Could I risk it and go to sleep again ? But if I did, wouldn't some neighbour find it before me ? Sheer predatory greed would then fling me out of the bed, and curiosity hurl me out into the cold, wet night. My flickering lantern would make the mist seem more solid. My feet grew eyes of their own and would lift me from rock to rock with a sleepwalker's sureness ; my hands, too, got to know the surface of the granite cliff with an almost indecent intimacy. I had become an addict. And the drug would send me slithering over the wet rocks every twelve hours, whatever the season, whatever the weather.

Many mornings, there was nothing but seaweed. On such days I would return home with only firewood and sit sullen through breakfast, having already exhausted myself before the day began. I would then resolve to give up this mad pursuit and get on with my work. Then just on the very next tide the sea would yield something to me as if unwilling to let me go. I remember the morning when I promised my wife I would go no more to the beach if there was nothing washed up by the next tide. But I knew there would be; I knew that the sea had no mercy.

The wind had been blowing from the south-west so, instead of going towards Gull Rock, I went towards Chizel Reach. As soon as I turned the point of the cove, I saw it. The tide had only just dropped it, its side was still flecked with foam. I raced across the rocks, terrified that the object for which I had waited and watched for so many tides might turn out to be a mirage, or, what would have been worse, be claimed by a neighbour getting his mark on it first.

But nobody was there before me. For a full minute I stood still, letting my eyes caress its lovely shape, appraising its full-bodied idol. I had dreamt it, wished it, willed it — this barrel. For this was no brewer's barrel which you often see rolled into a pub's cellar, but was the Emperor of all Barrels. I was reminded of a great ebony Buddha which had suddenly confronted me in an Indian jungle.

I tapped one end. It was full. If it had been empty, I know I would have wept with disappointment. But it was full. But full of what? Oil? Treacle? Pitch? Bran? What else goes in barrels? A panic of speculation seized me. I put my nose to it but could smell nothing, only the sea. Then I began grovelling for the bung and, breaking my pen-knife blade, gradually eased it out. A scarlet flow spurted into the night. It was as though I had let its blood; as if I had severed the artery of a wild boar. I put my mouth to it as one does to a fountain, and the wine gushed all over my neck. "My God!" I cried aloud, seldom feeling so fervent, "it's Burgundy!"

And I dived frantically to replace the bung. This secure, and my initials scratched on the end, I raced home across the rocks. As I went, I tried desperately to remember all the elementary mathematics I had learned at school in an effort to work out how much wine was in the barrel. The nearest I could get to the formula for volume was to remember the name of the master's wife . . . No matter, the problem was not to measure, but to salve, before the tide washed the barrel out again.

I ran upstairs to my wife who was still in bed. "Oh, what have you done ?" she cried, mistaking the wine on my shirt for blood.

"Quick! Quick!" I yelled, "give me a bottle; dozens of bottles," and, for a start, I grabbed her hot-water bottle and emptied it out of the window. Then I tore around the cottage, grabbing every jug, basin, pitch, pot or po.

All day, we went to the beach, back and forth, carrying our jars of wine until even the sink and the child's bath were full. At last, we counted eighty gallons of the sea's red mercy.

After this haul, there was no stopping me. And though no more wine came in, the sea kept me faithful to her tides by casting an occasional favour.

One morning, I found the beach simply littered with airtight tins — each full of American coffee in perfect condition. And, soon after the invasion of Normandy, two American supply ships collided in a fog off our coast. Like a greedy vulture, I waited.

Sometimes I had to wait a week, impatiently watching for the wind to change. When it did eventually, I found a man's leg lying on the beach. I knew the rest of the cargo would soon follow.

Sure enough, the next tide was profligate: cartons and crates were squandered on the shore. There must have been fifty thousand cigarettes, all perfectly dry. There were cigars, too. One could pick them out of the sea and light them, bless the packers. And all the comforts of bathroom culture followed, including hundreds of tubes of shaving cream, toothpaste, chewing gum, and, of course, contraceptives.

The village children used them as balloons and carried them gaily to school.

Then weeks would pass and I would find nothing but a mere slab of tallow, a dozen pit-props or a bale of raw rubber — for which the Custom and Excise would pay me £3 per bale.

And sometimes the tides would tease me pitilessly. I remember one sullen November, spending all the morning watching a barrel bob up and down on the backs of the waves. It seemed as if the tide just lacked sufficient strength to land it. I could tell it was full by the way it floated. I decided to wade out to it and push it ashore. I stripped, the water was maliciously cold. But I kept my eye on the barrel and waded on, up to my neck. Then I began to push the barrel ashore. Just as I had nearly succeeded in landing it, a great Atlantic roller came up behind me unawares and wrapped me helplessly round the barrel. As it turned, so did I too. And, in this ridiculous fashion, I rode the surf — with the slight difference of being underneath it. At last, the great wave flung us on to the beach: I, on top of my prize. Before I could break from this compulsory embrace, the wretched thing began to roll backwards over me. I turned, chasing it as it trundled faster and faster down the shingle, towards the sea again. Then a small rock arrested its mad career and I caught up with it, only to watch sixty gallons of Guinness seep into the thirsty sea . . . Few experiences have moved me as much as this did. I almost wept over the waste of it.

It is not that I like beer. I never drink it. But when the sea presents one with a gift, one is inclined to cast both taste and principles to the winds.

I remember some years ago that when a keg came in just below Hartland, it was picked up by a family of Wesleyan teetotallers. They abandoned their principles, and yielded to the temptation of drinking the wine. In spite of finding the taste rather bitter, they persisted and drank regularly with their meals rather than waste the stuff. Their reward for overcoming their prejudices was that their teeth gradually dissolved away in their mouths, which served them right, I suppose, for if they had known what good wine was, they would not have mistaken dilute hydrochloric acid for sauterne.

As we walked up the hill for the last time I noticed my shadow: the shoulders rounded from carrying great weights, but not sacks of wheat, and my legs like the staves of a barrel. As I say, it is not we who change a house of character — but it who alters us.

Now from my home at the top of the hill, I observe my tenant in the old mill in the throes of the same tyranny ; and I draw considerable satisfaction from the sight of him struggling daily under a load of driftwood as I leisurely sharpen my pencil.

But setting aside the lure of beachcombing, when anyone chooses to live in such a derelict house as I did, they do so probably because it is immensely satisfying to improve it ; and nothing is easier than to do that in North Devon or North Cornwall. The worst carpenter can find something there he is capable of repairing, and the laziest gardener soon sees signs of order where there was chaos and weeds before. Was that also my reason? I do not know. As usual, there is nothing for it but to write on, in order to discover what one knows but does not realize.

James Turner

Bodmin Moor

You will not like this shorn place unless your mind is attuned to the brilliance of loneliness and the hardness of nature. There is nothing of softness here unless it be the bogs and marshes all over the moor. A place, in its depths, inhabited only by cattle and horses, by wild bees in disused quarries, and the mounting skylark. A place lit by the light of wide skies and the colours of yellow lichen, milkwort, biting-stone-crop and the green of open space. A forgotten place of ruined cottages on the edge of civilization, crossed by horse riders, and a single jet plane overhead. A place of profound secrets and of revitalizing myth.

We have forgotten the importance of myth. We need such a place as Bodmin Moor to reveal ourselves to ourselves. Yet it will not receive you in a single visit, and you need humility and courage to face this truth. You are broken down before it. And then surviving, you are built up again under its fierce healing power. Here is the last silence of pools and the haunts of neolithic civilization, when man had not lost touch with nature, and spoke the language of cattle and grasses. And came to the green sedges and grey cromlechs to die and be buried in the nature he understood.

Wide over all is the expanded sky about the church towers and the clapper bridges, like those at Bradford, where at mid-day, the bulls come down to drink and to shake off the flies. They stand knee-deep in the cool waters of the De Lank river below the waterworks and seem to be listening to the chittering of a wren in the hedge opposite. The lush watermeadows are polished with buttercup, the may scent is heady over the walls of fallen farm buildings. The skies of the moor are the monopoly of God in summer or the wrath of His displeasure in winter, under snow, when the moor is full of tiny explosions of grasses, brittle and snapping under the weight of thawing frost. Grasses burnt by a one-eyed sun in the long days of August; the ash of grass in the sweeping salt gales of winter.

In this area of thin earth over granite are the faggots of history before history, amid the rough envelopes of moorland parishes. Fields stolen from rocks and rock-burdened still, full of the last remnants of copper and tin mines, the chimneys of their ruined engine houses upthrust against the modern television tower at Caradon Hill. Such ruins are the pathetic reminders of an early industrial age.

You walk on the diagram of a railway line from the pub at St. Cleer, to the immense mouthful of the Cheesewring quarries. This is a granite landscape, and the traces of the railway (there are no lines now) are those of the Cheesewring line, running down from the disused quarry to Caradon and Liskeard. It was opened in November, 1844 and, two years later, it was extended into the moor to serve the quarries, and the Kilmar granite quarries beyond. It was a gravity line, standard gauge, the trucks, full of iron ore, being returned when empty by horses. Before 1860, when passenger coaches were attached to the line, people could always get a seat in the 'mineral' waggons, by a free pass, if they paid for a parcel. Many of the inhabitants of the now deserted little hamlets must have so travelled to their shopping in Liskeard. The railway was abandoned on 31st December, 1916. The great days of the mines and quarries had passed. We are left with this trace of a railway line in the landscape dominated by the Cheesewring, forever toppling and never falling, the Turk's stone-cap pointing to the interior.

The setting out from the Cheesewring itself is like advancing into a sea of grass and deepset stones with the heights of Brown Willy beckoning you on into the wilderness, to the long shales of its lower slopes. Behind you are The Hurlers on their green lawn, those upright stones which are supposed to be Sunday dancers ossified for their evil ways. Whatever the mystery of them, they stand now immobile, decade after decade, watching posts for the stonechat and crow, as ungiving of their secrets as the great burial chamber, the Quoit at Trethevy, a little way off, of the Minions and the Celtic cross on the avenue of roads into the moor.

Immediately before you is a ruined farmhouse in the waste of stone and stone hedges, being sucked backed into the moor by time. In the calm heat of a summer's day you can hear that 'winged chariot' with its blazing horses, charging from the quarry heights, and hear again the agonised lowing and bellowing of the bull which was once chained in the bull-house beside the farm itself, now given over, in its lower rooms, to fostering cattle against winter. Amongst the litter on the stone floors are the pages of a copy of 'The News of the World' for 1922. The empty oven holds the charred sticks of the fire which baked the last loaf of bread to be eaten here, when those who were leaving forever were packed and ready to go back off the moor and the hardness of their life. Such ruins epitomise the falling-into-nature of the moor. They are the modern scratchings of human beings who have failed, down the centuries, to leave anything but etchings on the moor itself.

From the hot summer stones (what Ice Age deposited them?) the chalk blue butterfly rises, the dragon fly basks in the arbours of its greenness, the bracken seen through its diaphanous wings. A slow worm wriggles away between the dry stalks of grass hummocks, swimming in grass. There is nothing but silence. In the bird's wing of this blue day, the deep places of the moor are born. They are no different from neolithic times; only we are that.

You follow the river Fowey, here small and rushy, between Smallcombe Downs and Browngelly Downs until you come from the silence to the hiss of the A30, the great moor road, to Bolventor and Jamaica Inn. And you pass them to stay beside the little inland lake of Dozmary Pool where King Arthur gave

Sir Bedivere his sword Excalibur to cast away. At the poolside he heard

> the ripple washing on the reeds
> And the wild water lapping on the crag,

and finally cast away, after the third time of asking, the magic sword. It was the end.

> Then quickly rose Sir Bedivere, and ran
> And, leaping down the ridges lightly, plunged
> Among the bull-rush beds, and clutch'd the sword
> And strongly wheel'd and threw it. The great brand
> Made flashings in the splendour of the moon
> And flashing round and round, and whirl'd in an arch
> Shot like a streamer of the northern morn,
> Seen where the moving isles of winter shock
> By night, with noises of the Northern Sea.
> So flash'd and fell the brand Excalibur ;
> But ere he dipped the surface, rose an arm
> Clothed in white samite, mystic, wonderful,
> And caught him by the hilt, and brandish'd him
> Three times, and drew him under in the mere.

> > The Passing of Arthur. Tennyson.

And so, this being done, Arthur was carried, dying, to the barge and the three Queens who awaited him. As it disappeared into the mist over Dozmary Pool (or, perhaps Loe Pool, who can tell ?) the great Cornish legend of Arthur was born, the King whose soul passed into the body of a chough. When you stand alone by this evening water, you can believe it. The cattle come in to drink from Deweymeads and Gilhouse, from the neolithic hut circles under Harrowbridge Hill. To the south is the little lost hamlet of Temple, overshadowed to the north west by china clay pyramids.

Here, in the 12th century, the Knights Templar held a small area of Bodmin Moor. Here they had a church and a 'commandery.' When the Order was suppressed, in 1314, the Knights Hospitallers came into the property. In 1340, in order to give hospitality to passers-by, a preceptor, one brother, and two servants lived here with a chaplain. From about 1744 Temple became famous as a sort of Gretna Green, where all ' sorts of irregularities were carried out with impunity.' Carew, the historian, wrote that 'many a bad marriage is there yearly slubbered up.' The church was in ruins in the 1800's. It was rebuilt in 1883, but has now been declared 'redundant' and closed.

To be in the hamlet of Temple is like being in the Midlands at the time when the Deserted villages were on their last legs. Ash, sycamore, oak and elm hedge-in the falling houses, owls call from the stone roof angles. A few more years and time will have dragged it back to the desolation of the neolithic hut circles about it. Or it will be swallowed up in the industry of Bodmin itself, or sucked down into the nearby bogs of Menridden and Stiffles.

If always Brown Willy and Rough Tor draw you into the moor, there are other ways than their lower slopes to enter. St. Breward is a village high on the edge of the moor, an outpost of grey Cornish stone cottages, a pub and a church in which is the carved slate, showing a former vicar, in 1607, Lewis Adams, his wife in a high-crowned hat and full-skirted gown, kneeling behind him. 'This worke,' says the inscription, 'was made at the cost of John Adams, his sonne, in 1609.'

These moorland villages have about them a closed-in air, self-sufficient, standing upon the hopes of ancient cultures, steadfast, indestructible. Their lanes are often full of cattle ; farms are at their centre and the sheep dog growls in the hot sun, guarding a memory as old as the moor. Pack horses crossed the clapper (from Latin clapperius, great stone) bridges laden with ribbons and trifles for Launceston Fair or Liskeard market, or Bodmin, their long legs reflected in the water of strong, still streams, peaty and brown, down moorland chines.

From St. Breward lead off a number of roads into the moor. Once on the moor itself they peter out into the traces of the old trading tracks which ran northward to the Midlands and north west to Wales. One of these lanes leads to the De Lank Water-works, discreetly hidden above the small clapper bridge over the stream. To the right, also hidden from the bridge, are the quarries at Hante-Gantick, in the rock grandeur of its valley, and the Hannon valley, where two moorland crags, the Devil's Jump, flank a ravine.

Leaze cottage stands on the edge of the moor, raised up from amongst the great stones where sheep shelter in winter, not far from King Arthur's Hall. Anything out-of-the-ordinary in Cornwall is labelled with Arthur's name, from Tintagel to mysterious heaps of stones. This large open space surrounded by stones (you can see indeed, that it was once a 'hall' or meeting place, or store) was built by the Beaker folk when they came into Cornwall from Wiltshire. They used it for a store-house. All Cornwall from Chysauster, near Penzance, with its clearly defined village, to Bodmin Moor, with its stone and hut circles was populated by these people in about 2,000 B.C. Even then the citadels of Rough Tor and Brown Willy must have seemed inpregnable fortresses to them, or god-places, the sun spinning off their summits in summer ; the moon, in winter, split by the ragged granite. To such people these mighty hills were their 'history,' pin-pointed on the map of their descent.

Above Leaze cottage is a small stone quarry, unused for a hundred years, where pools of greenish water create, in spring, tiny gardens of wild rock plants in full flower. Below this quarry with its split granite blocks still shaped and left, is a perfect stone circle which must have been connected with the great store house at King Arthur's Hall. The sun roasts their unreadable signatures. You can stand in the centre of this circle, the long grass above your ankles, and it is easy to imagine such 'temples' filled. Was the sun both their god and their magic? One thing is certain, they must have carried water up from the De Lank river, and bought their fish from other Beaker folk who lived beside the sea at such places as Harlyn Bay and, perhaps, came carrying bass and herring, lobster and crab inland to sell. To them, as to us to-day, the leviathans of Bodmin Moor's two mountains would seem to be moving under the sun's shadow, and God to speak out of the clouds which came inland to enclose their summits.

They would have carried their dead to tumuli, in the burial grounds beyond their hearths. What language did these people speak to each other ? In the silence of present-day moorland you can still catch faint murmurings of their voices from the stones which they raised and the stone fire-places of their almost disintegrated homes, so little has changed in the remote wards of Bodmin Moor.

With the De Lank river behind you, you can walk to another cottage at Mount Pleasant, rarely used except in summer, with Garrow Tor rising before you, with its lonely shepherd's hut, a kind of entrée to Brown Willy beyond. Garrow is dotted with hut circles about King Arthur's Downs. And so, by the valley stream which feeds the river, by cattle-tongue and the spring flower, to the slopes of the mountain. Between the two mountains stands a roofed hut by the stream. It is said to be the place where St. Petroc settled.

Upon the summit of Rough Tor you seem to be standing at the heart of Cornwall, with the land spread out below you, the sea on both sides of you and Dartmoor in the distance. You are pin-pointed on a large scale Ordnance Survey map of landscape, the centre of a topographical puzzle completed and all pieces in place since the world began. To the north west are the great cliffs at Crackington Haven. There is Beeny Cliff, near Boscastle, where Thomas Hardy courted Emma Gifford, who lived at the rectory of St. Juliot, the church which Hardy came, as a young man, to restore. To the south east, across the brown wastes of the moor, are the great china clay pits about St. Austell, and the rivers running white with clay effluent, right to Carlyon Bay. As the land narrows like a pencil you seem able to see even the Scillies.

There are other ways into the moor, through the doors of its deeply tunnelled lanes, down the long strides of Altarnun and the great woods and valleys of North Hill. The church at Altarnun is the glory of Bodmin Moor, the tower tall and pinnacled and built of surface granite from the moor itself. Here, too, is the Georgian Wesleyan Chapel. Over the door is the effigy of John Wesley, carved by Nevill Northey Burnard, the Cornish sculptor, who became famous and died in poverty. Charles Causley has celebrated him in a fine poem.

Two stone bridges cross Penpont Water, below the church, and the stream leads backwards, through fields and farms to the slopes of Bray Down and Buttern Hill. Now Brown Willy is to the south, dominating the scenery. So the moor is bounded and edged and rimmed by the soft villages and meadows. It waits to reveal itself beyond hawthorn hedges and in the cemented roof-tiles of hedge farms, with honey for sale, and the bold horns of

28

THE CLAW OF CORNWALL: ". . . the forbidding grandeur of the coast-line about Land's End . . ."

THE CLAW OF CORNWALL: "... gulls that piloted ..."

THE CLAW OF CORNWALL: ". . . still aloof and rather splendidly detached from the activity across Tamar hailed as progress."

ONE FOOT IN EITHER COUNTY: "The tide never turned but I was there to meet it. And the tide turns twice a day."

BODMIN MOOR: "A place of profound secrets and revitalizing myth."

BODINNICK-by-FOWEY: "And my bit of Cornwall is the village of Bodinnick, a small slice of magic, where a one-time boat-yard is my haven."

CORNWALL FROM THE SEA: ''Cornwall has little to offer in the way of shelter . . . only Fowey . . .''

THE CHINA CLAY COUNTRY: "My Cornwall is different, at once starkly modern and more radically mystical."

bulls who peer at you over the granite escutcheons of the outcrop of moorland, inviting you to enter through the gates or dolmens and border grass, challenging you to the effort of the moor, and the hard-booted walking over shale to the summits.

If Altarnun is the glory of the moor's edge, then St. Clether, with its holy well and chapel to the saint is the most touching memorial on the moor. It is the moor's gentleness, one of its great places, hallowed by the Saint's halo. It stands beside the river Inny where it runs in a deep valley from Davidstow Moor until, miles later, it joins the Tamar beyond Lezant. You can take the hardness, the loneliness, the implacability of the moor to St. Clether and receive back its gentleness. The bold nakedness of the moor, which shrivels the soul into blackness and whitens it again in its own time, has given place here to the softness of moor stream and the heron fishing. But yet, in the great boulders, like houses, which emerge from the sides of the valley, the feeling, the aspect of moorland is not far away. The Saint's singing echoed down the hollowness of these hills to the village a mile away. Beyond the day when these huge stones came bowling down off the moor heights, this ancient land stood and welcomed the Saint as he came to the valley and saw the water springing from the rock and knew his place forever.

'There are more Saints in Cornwall than in Heaven,' it is often said. Most of them were early Christian missionaries who came into Cornwall in the 5th and 6th centuries A.D. They often took over the existing tribal system and preached from the many pre-Christian crosses still to be seen. Besides these bare emblems their white beards waved in the Cornish winds, their tongues tasted the salt blown inland from the sea and their gnarled hands baptized the hard granite. In their mouths was love, and the food their disciples brought them. Their crosses were both their altars and their restaurants, and the fountains gushed permanently over their feet, and in and out of their grass fonts.

They built baptisteries over the sacred fountains where the people had worshipped before they came. These springs now became Holy Wells, their waters having mysterious and wonderful powers. There are some hundred and fifty Holy Wells, or sites of Holy Wells, in Cornwall. All of them had their particular virtues, apart from curing sore eyes and whooping cough and rickets. For example, if you wanted to find out how your absent friends were getting on you made a pilgrimage to St. Gulval's Well, at Penzance, and made the appropriate prayers over the bubbling water. If you wanted to insure against your child being hanged, you had it baptized with water from Venton-Uny Well, near Redruth. If you wanted to cure a madman you bowssened (or dipped) him in St. Nona's Well, at Altarnun.

St. Clether's Well is one of the great Cornish Wells. It is some way from the church, but the walk to it is a delightful expedition on a summer's evening. The church was originally Norman. The earliest record of it is its consecration, by Bishop Bronescombe of Exeter, on October 23rd, 1259. After the Reformation, the church gradually fell into decay until, in 1865, it was entirely rebuilt and most of the Norman features which, to-day, we should treasure, were ' ironed out.'

The walk to St. Clether's Well is, in every sense, a pilgrimage to a Holy Place. By the church stile, sticks are provided to help pilgrims along the half mile of green valley. Before you as you go over the fields, the roof of the Chapel appears in the distance, above the river. All this part of the valley is in fact, called Chapel Park. How easy it is to imagine St. Clether, son of a Welsh chieftain, coming over the hill in front of you, sometime towards the end of the 5th century A.D., rejoicing in the sight of the water bubbling from the rock !

And so he built his holy place for healing, this well, and his chapel for prayer and contemplation. The people came to him with food, to be healed, and he fished in the river Inny and, in winter lay down with the sheep for warmth until he died, ' at an advanced age,' and was buried somewhere about here. His chapel fell into ruin, and it was not until 1895 that the building was restored by the Rev. S. Baring Gould, who did so much for Cornwall. Only the floor plan remained when he arrived, the foundations going back more than a thousand years. It was necessary to rebuild the upper parts of the walls and re-roof the building which was dedicated in 1900. Services are held here occasionally and, it is said that Baring Gould gave all the royalties on his hymn ' Onward Christian Soldiers ' to pay for the restoration.

Inside the chapel the water, from the well in the rocks outside, passes under the altar and then into a recess in the south wall also outside. There is a shelf above this second well where, it is supposed, pilgrims left their offerings. Below this pre-Reformation altar is a recess which may well have held relics of the Saint. The water running by was probably doubly sanctified by such relics.

We used to come, when we were boys, for holidays to Mr. Old's farmhouse on Pentire Point in the late '20's' and early '30's.' We came from London and, naturally, we came for the sea, the caves, the loneliness of such places as the beach at The Strangles. Yet I only had to look backwards from the heights of Crackington Haven and there were the wide stretches of Bodmin Moor, dominated by its twin mountains. But we never went there, except that on the way down and back again, we crossed the moor in the three-seater Citroen car belonging to my brother Jack. I'm convinced now, that as we sped up the long road to Launceston, we all closed our eyes against the bleakness on either hand.

It was a mistake ; we missed what to me is, now, the finest part of Cornwall. We missed the wonderful stained glass in St. Neot's church, and the wide sweeps of Cardinham Moor south of the great stretches of the main moorland. Perhaps we were too young, then, to appreciate the experience, physical and spiritual, of the moor places where the birds sing with more ecstacy and the buzzards stand taller to the wind. I was not ready, then, as I have been since, to confront the wolf and the bear in their stone caves. To have looked at the mask of a fox in Sydney Woods, in Kent, near my home was enough.

Camelford is one of the moor towns. A long lane leads up to the foot of Rough Tor which you can climb if you've a mind to, and so over open moorland, and up Brown Willy. Now-a-days I have come to agree with G. K. Chesterton that 'mountains exist to be looked up at, not down from.' Beyond the town, some three miles, is a turning which takes you to Davidstow, where the Americans had an aerodrome during the last war which was rarely used because of driving sea mists. Indeed, now the sea is not far off. You scent the salt in the air as you cross the fields to the lonely church of St. Adwena, at Advent. Here they are laid, down the centuries, the skeletons beneath these slabs, communing in the dusklight. Why should they not ? There is no one else to talk to, as the meadows fill with the yellow light of buttercups and the daisies close. What must they think of the occasional visitor ? They scuttle back beneath their slate shells and whisper to one another ;

As we are, so shalt thou be.

The long road from Davidstow drives towards Launceston, through State forests of pines on the left. Just before Wilsey Down forest you turn off into the parish of Davidstow which is full of stone lanes and lovely names such as Lambrenny, Treglasta, Woolgarden, Trevillan's Gate and Doney's Shop, and come south to Rough Tor again over Davidstow Moor, between the great Crowdy Marsh, into Lowermoor and the mountain itself, and beyond the china clay pits at Stannon Downs. It is a picture you can hold in your hands, framed by the small towns and the gracious, unbending churches until you come to Bodmin itself.

Bodmin is a dark town, overlaid by pain and sorrow. The gaol stands in a hollow to the north-west and, though it is closed it is a kind of ' fate ' over the long town street, the small cottages, the narrow lanes, which it will never throw off. It is the same with all gaol towns. It possesses a human shame not made any better by turning the gaol into a Night Club and allowing people to drink cocktails in the condemned cell. Human misery is not washed out in gin, like this. So that Bodmin is a town for early morning. Seen then, from Cardinham Moor, in the rising sun in its valley, it is like a brown jewel. Seen from Cardinham with its two ancient Celtic crosses and its blackberry fields. Behind Bodmin are the woods of Lanhydrock framing the town.

But now, in autumn, the sun shines upon the altar tomb of Prior Vyvyan, who died in 1533 It is made of dark blue Catacleuse slate, with its vested effigy on top. The sun glows upon the slate in Bodmin church warming it with the last of summer. Warming, too the elvan stone of the small town cottages up Fore Street. Now, before the lorries have begun their parade up the A30, there is nothing in the streets but a cat going from one house to another between the main street and the ring road, stopping for a moment to drink from the little well above the car park with its legend EYE WATER. Was this some healing well like that of Saint Guron west of the church ? High on the far hill is the monument erected to commemorate Sir Walter Raleigh Gilbert who was born in Bodmin, and created a baronet for his services in the British Army in India. The hangman could see the tip of it as he knotted the rope round a victim's neck and laid his drop.

Some absurd memorials, such miseries, are forgotten in the long night of the autumn moor. Already the hollows beneath the stone plinths are beginning to turn purple, the few gorse flowers to swell into yellow globes, dying in the last of the night, as the moon comes riding up over the sea above this vast granite shelf, and whirls skydown between St. Agnes Head and into the Edwardian terraces of Bude. It crosses the shadow of night birds. The owl hoots from windshorn branches of a meagre tree, its noise only increasing the silence below the curious stones of the Cheesewring. When the moon rolls down between the mountains (backwards and forwards it seems to go, up one side, down one side, up one side) the granite splits into fragments, borne deep into the chalice of the moor, splintered on horned cattle and lowly weeds, rest-harrow and self-heal and scarlet pimpernel.

It begins to be cold ; heat is being withdrawn from the long moor meadows. Sheep pull their long fleeces about them. a slight wind blows into and out of the holes of stones and disturbs the green algae on the secret pools. The night begins a low whistling on Garrow Tor, winding up the spindles of marsh reeds and the great clocks of dandelion seed float outwards from the gardens of Camelford and Launceston, of Wadebridge and Bodmin. The day's last beetle bangs its horned case down the corridor of Shallow Water Common under Hawk's Tor and the mist floats, like a handkerchief, over Dozmary Pool where, they say, the giant Tregeagle is still trying, after centuries of punishment, to bail out the water with a leaky limpet shell.

Under the night hours the moor increases, the mountains become taller, more majestic, dangerous, spirit-inhabited. The sound of the sea is clear, running over the sands of The Strangles, and the moorland seems to slip away to meet it as you wait for the sun to rise and the whole land to breathe again in the pink light. Colour is coming back into nature.

33

4

Angela du Maurier

Fowey

What indeed is my Cornwall ? This evening it is sitting by an open door with silver-grey water lapping a few feet beneath me. I am listening to music — a passion of mine — the Beethoven Violin Concerto. Everything is pale grey, the evening sky, the lapping water, the distant houses of Polruan — even three small gulls which were hatched a few weeks ago on the rocks beside my house, and whose parents come into the kitchen and steal the cat's dinner. It is evening, my favourite time of the day. Visitors — ' trippers ' — have gone, the noisy ferry has stopped. The little fleet of sailing ' Troys ' have packed up, I'm alone with the beauty of Fowey harbour which captivated my family nearly half a century ago. My Cornwall ? The tiny church of St. John the Baptist in Bodinnick (my village) where I go weekly to Mass and keep the altar linen clean, and am in fact the sacristan. My Cornwall ? Another Church, that of St. Winnow, a few miles up the Fowey river where I hope one day to rest my earthly remains. St. Winnow lies by the river banks — alive or dead I must be near water it seems. From my bedroom window if I were brave enough and a good enough diver, I could throw myself out into the water beneath. Big ships from foreign parts drop anchor at night when I'm reading in bed — ships from Russia, Roumania, Spain, Holland, Germany, and I leap from my bed and peer through the window always wondering if they will — by mistake — crash into the slipway of my home and demolish house and me at one fell swoop. My Cornwall ? A walk to Pencarrow when the gorse is in bloom, Lantic Bay to my right, Lantivet to my left. A summer's day with the lark singing overhead. Lanes — quiet lanes free from tourists, leading to little Pont Creek, or a lane without a name that wanders toward Tywardreath, it is off the beaten track and passes one ivy-covered farmhouse. Bluebells ; surely nowhere but in Cornwall are there such seas of bluebells ? See them in the woods of Lanhydrock, or Golitha ; in the hedgerows in nearby lanes. Bluebells, primroses, foxgloves — Cornwall has them in unlimited profusion and beauty.

Villages that I love and small towns like Lostwithiel, Lerryn, Fowey, Lanreath, Polruan, Polkerris — and those further afield, St. Mawes, Padstow, Truro.

I was eight years old when I first fell in love with Cornwall, Mullion Cove. My parents took a hideous bungalow for the summer holiday, they hated it and left almost immediately for France but my sisters with a nanny remained, and I thought it the most beautiful and romantic place in the world. Then aged 13 after a bad attack of measles, we all went to Kennack, in those days only sharing the magnificent sands with cattle, and it was many years later we found Fowey. London born and bred I am constantly asked how it was that I have put down my roots. I don't like cities, not to live in. London is not what it was when I was young, and I think London is for the young and for the worker, the worker whose work is there. I happen to be a lover of beauty, whether that beauty is Fowey harbour, the Cornish moors, the lakes of Westmorland and Cumberland, Tresco, Connemara, or the Italian Dolomites. I'm lucky enough to live by the water's edge in Fowey harbour, and do not want to live anywhere else. Local interests are mine, whether they are concerned with the church, politics, various charities — dearly loved friends are near me.

An hour or more has passed, and the lights are now glimmering in Polruan, the water has reached the grass, a small row boat has passed and a neighbour has waved ; the swish of the waves behind me and the Schubert Octet are the only sounds ; clouds are parting and soon the full moon will appear ; maybe the light under which I'm writing will attract a bat ; the three tiny gulls are slowly drifting towards me, it is time for them to go to bed. How could I live anywhere else ? This is my Cornwall.

Alone in my little rather unsafe boat, or in my car, I can be happy drinking in the remaining beauty of this county. I say remaining because a lot of it has indeed been very spoiled, and many hideous buildings have been erected, and pretty villages are fast losing their ancient charm. Was there ever — is there — a county that is so varied ? The clay district which has a gaunt fascination of its own — one either acknowledges its strange beauty or hates it ; the barren cliffs of Tintagel ; the soft almost sub-tropical country around Falmouth ; the bleak exciting moors with Rough Tor and Brown Willy ; our commercialized but still entrancingly pretty villages such as Polperro, Mevagissey and Looe ; but many though there be I still would give the prize to Fowey, Q's Troy Town.

Now it is a late August evening . . . high tide . . . All the afternoon I've dealt with a stall for our Lanteglos Parish Church fête, in superb sunshine. Then, later, something I enjoy doing more than anything else in Cornwall ; an evening row in my cockleshell of a boat. Sometimes I think that is my Cornwall: rowing, entirely alone, up Pont Creek which is quite beautiful and unspoilt . . . a kingfisher darts along the bank, and gulls who have forsaken cliffs for riverside nests view me with a certain amount of suspicion. Then back to my house, my home, a well-earned (?) drink, and I sit down by the so-called stable-door, a few feet from the water's edge, and as I look across the changing colours of the harbour I know that I could live nowhere else, unless — possibly — in the fells of Cumberland, where mountains as well as water give me all I can ask.

How I love my Cornish gulls, who sleep with heads tucked under the wing, or else before ' turning in ' appear to sit on the water in rows ; black-backed, herring-gulls, kittiwakes, black-headed. From my stable-door the sun sets behind trees immediately opposite me — this evening the clouds look like Greek islands in a golden sea.

My Cornwall ? At all seasons of the year it is the world I am happy in which to live. A small world perhaps, one that many town-livers would consider too parochial, possibly too

36

self-centred. But is it ? In our small villages and townships world disasters do not pass us by ; coffee-mornings, bazaars, fêtes, Bingo-evenings, wine & cheese parties, even concerts are held week in week out for all the deserving causes of which we neither can escape hearing or reading about, even if we wished.

Churches of Cornwall play a big part in my own love of the county. Apart from whatever one's own religion is I here mean the buildings themselves, and I am proud to have played a small part in fêtes which I have opened for them, fêtes to raise money to keep these so beautiful medieval places of worship going, for it is a never ending war against the ravages of time, and death-watch beetles, and decaying fabric. I have already spoken of St. Winnow's Church, and ' my ' tiny St. John's ; but those at Lanreath, Lansallos, Duloe, Talland, St. Veep — all near to me, all 14th century or older, are quite lovely. Small Golant church with exquisitely carved pews, the church of Hyacinth of Blisland (one of the most beautiful in the country) ; St. Endellion ; St. Just-in-Roseland, entry to which means descent through a sub-tropical garden filled with camellias, mimosas, eucalyptus and the bluest of hydrangeas ; I call it a garden, church-yard or cemetery would seem a wrong nomenclature. And then there is St. Ewe, in a tiny unspoilt village, St. Ewe Church where one Easter I found a perfect Easter Morning Garden laid inside the church, laid in miniature, the Open Sepulchre was fashioned from stones brought in from outside, and there were two minute angels, primroses and other wild flowers were scattered nearby. My own parish church of Lanteglos-by-Fowey is one of the most beautiful ; my sister was married there one early morning many years ago and her two daughters christened there. It lies rather isolated by a farmhouse, as many other Cornish churches do. At Christmas we have midnight Mass there when the church is lit solely by candles, candles in the window sills, candles in the pews, many candles on the altar, I go with two friends every year to prepare and light them. St. Cubert is another lovely little church in a strange village, a church which is reminiscent of some northern French village place of worship ; St. Neot, with outstanding glass, it is said to have some of the most beautiful remaining medieval glass in a parish church in the country. These are village churches, and Bodinnick's small St. John's is so dear to me because it was converted from an old stable only since the last war, and was intended for the old people of the village, of whom there were then a good many, and all of us helped in the making. Cornwall's larger churches, those of Fowey, Bodmin, St. Germans, St. Ives, Launceston, are all beautiful, many with ancient monuments to old departed medieval families, little stone figures of kneeling gallants and their ladies, often in Elizabethan garb, ruffs round their necks, with probably a collection of offspring kneeling beside them ; and superbly carved pews and rood-screens can be found in a great many of these churches, and relics of the Civil War too.

Buildings — Houses. One has to admit that as far as beautiful villages are concerned Cornwall cannot compete with the Cotswold country, or some in unspoilt Kent. This is probably because Cornwall's coastline is so lovely that Man in his usual iconoclastic way has done his best during this century to plaster the ' delectable duchy ' with as many undelectable buildings as he can in order, one can only suppose, for as many people who can to holiday in. But there are still beautiful houses in Cornwall, old houses still lived in by families who have owned them for generations. Place, at Fowey ; Boconnoc ; Trelowarren ; Port Eliot ; Lanhydrock (now National Trust) ; Penheale Manor ; Menabilly. These are houses I know or have known, there are countless others but it is my Cornwall that I am writing about so I must only write of people, places and things I know.

Houses : my own house, once a boat-builder's yard, my family (my mother, my sisters and I), discovered it with a ' For Sale ' board outside it some 45 years ago. A stream ran through the mud floor of what is now a large (and I think heavenly!) living-room ; 3 bedrooms and a bathroom are where once was a sail-loft, and of course no stair-case led to it in those days ; and the top floor was the one and only habitable part of the dwelling, which was — and is — completely self-contained. Deeds show that the lower part of the thick-walled house are many hundreds of years old, the top of course was added. ' Built against the country ' as they say down here, rock bursts through and in fact is, the fourth wall of the house. Sometimes after a spell of much rain, water trickles down the walls of the rock-face, but by a clever architectural feat continues its way under the house to the sea, and the house is never damp. Ferryside is in fact my Cornwall.

And what do I do here in my Cornwall ? The years have passed, more than forty-five of them, since I came as a fairly young person in my twenties, to spend casual weeks in the summer-time, at Easter, at Christmas ; for 'holidays,' away from the rush, bustle and enjoyment of London life. My Cornwall then was very different ; it meant house-parties with one's parents' friends, it meant London's house-staff of maids, it meant several boats, (with someone in daily attendance), it meant day-long picnics at Pridmouth or Lantivet, it meant wonderful walks with lots of dogs. And it meant very scant knowledge of what Cornwall was going to mean to me as like the Ten Little Nigger Boys one by one each member of the family toppled away and now here I am, alone, ' Miss Angela ' to the village, a Senior Citizen (i.e. Old Age Pensioner) with a small cat as company, — beloved dogs lie in their graves in the garden. My Cornwall is now being ' on ' This & That ; of having many interests from which forty years ago I would have shrunk. It means that instead of a garden party at Buckingham Palace (to which I used to go when my father was alive) I go to the Polruan Vicarage for our parish fête ; it means I am actually a churchwarden instead of playing the part of Wendy in Peter Pan ; it means an active part in branch (Conservative) politics instead of pompously proclaiming myself a socialist (after helping in the out-patients department in one of the big London hospitals as a very inadequate V.A.D.). It means in 1971 a life of content as far as one can be content with world horrors growing apace and only a few people like Mother Theresa to inspire one. Voltaire it was (I think) who said ' Cultivate one's garden,' and I don't even do that as well as I might.

Gardens. The glory of Cornwall's gardens in May and June can only be realised by those lucky enough to see them. Tregrehan's camellias, the rhododendrons of Trewithen, the magic of Lanhydrock when magnolias are in bloom, the unbelievable romance of Caerhays . . . giant magnolias and azaleas standing as sentinels behind the castle looking like something from a fairy story with the lake beneath. Sentinels : there are places in Cornwall where fox-gloves stand like regiments of sentinels. There is a bank near Lostwithiel close to lovely Pelyn House where foxgloves stand like guardsmen and I remember a lane leading to Lamorna where they must have been growing in their thousands. There are parts of Cornwall which I cannot in all conscience call 'mine,' it would be presumptuous; they are just 'bits' that I wish were nearer to and could visit oftener. The moor, — Bodmin Moor — wild, exciting, less known than Dartmoor and Exmoor, smaller of course, but just because of this better loved by many Cornish people. Dozmare pool in which, so legend says, Arthur flung Excalibur — Brown Willy and Rough Tor can be climbed with comparative ease and the smell of peat wafts to one's nostrils and is there for the digging (if you know where to find it). There is Davidstow Moor too, which few people seem to know; the last war's forsaken planes' hangars now stand derelict, the whole area a place for sheep to wander at will; and not far away is the church of Altarnun, the Cathedral of the moor, one of the most beautiful of all Cornwall's churches. Tintagel is far from Bodinnick, but I have taken people to look and wonder at what remains of Arthur's castle; much nearer, by the Fowey river, are woods where Tristan and Isolde wooed, herons and curlews have their haunts there nowadays. My Cornwall should be Fowey itself. How many people are there, people in other parts of the peninsula, who do not realise that Fowey also means Polruan, Mixtow, Bodinnick, the whole 'country' parish of Lanteglos? Lanteglos-by-Fowey not to be confused with Lanteglos-by-Camelford. Here, on the eastern shores of the Fowey river, our postal address is Fowey, our telephone numbers are Polruan, we pay our rates to Liskeard, our member of Parliament belongs to the Bodmin Division, our nearest station is Lostwithiel! And Lostwithiel is one of my favourite small towns, with a plethora of old buildings. The Fowey river by-passes the village and the ancient stronghold of Restormel stands high on the hill a mile away. It is such a friendly little town with its ancient church of St. Bartholomew, nestling as it seems to in a basin of land mid-way between Liskeard, Bodmin and St. Austell.

To return to the inhabitants — myself among them — of Fowey (both sides of the river). One cannot say there is rivalry between the people of Fowey, Polruan & Bodinnick, but none of us ever wish to change places and live in either of the other two. Fowey people imagine the tie of having to cross by a ferry to either Polruan or Bodinnick to be insupportable. We in Bodinnick snap our fingers over that nuisance while congratulating ourselves that the East Wind which so often makes Fowey many degrees colder than our side, never touches us, nestling as we do under the hill which protects us. Polruan is more or less self-supporting, we in Bodinnick are not, there is not a shop in the place, not so much as a stamp machine. So most of us know Fowey a great deal better than the people of Fowey know us and our houses and cottages. We take the often long wait for the ferry in our stride and know in our hearts that it helps to keep our precious near-isolation a few years longer, for a bridge can never be built thanks to the ships which pass up by us to the jetties for their china clay cargoes.

To live in Fowey by the water's edge as I do is a constant source of interest, ships are romantic even though the days of sail are long past. In the years that I have lived here I have seen many changes in their nationalities. Before the war the great Maru's from Japan passed by our windows, and small British coasters — 'Rose' boats they were — and Dutch ships whose names always ended in 'stroom.' We knew them all. Tugs have changed as well, the small Countess of Jersey was greatly loved. Maybe she and others like her helped in the evacuation from Dunkirk.

War years. I remember thinking the thing I would care most to see would be the twinkling lights of the harbour once again. Before D-Day our harbour was filled with American ships, flat bottomed troop carriers and others. For some months we were a base for the American navy. And then one day the harbour was empty ; it had happened ; the Normandy beaches were once again to be trodden by Allied feet. And now ships of many countries glide by this house, small ships and quite big merchantmen, eleven thousand tonners . . . from Russia, from Roumania, from Panama . . . an occasional Israeli, many from Spain, the Scandinavian countries, Germany, Holland. Fowey people love their port and are proud of the fact that it carries the county's china clay all over the world. Its sister port of Par takes smaller ships, and a fascinating picture is that of perhaps a dozen little ships at anchor in Par Bay waiting for the tide to enable them to make the entry into Par Harbour. Cargo ships are not the only vessels, for Fowey is a great centre for yachts and in the summer sails of every colour and kind can be seen. Sometimes I do wonder why I love living in surroundings so utterly unlike those in which I was brought up, the more so as the usual country pursuits are not mine. I could never have hunted, (the horse has not been born off which I'd not have fallen), I am indeed timid of quite a lot of animals and have been known to walk miles rather than go through a field of cattle, and on-coming geese fill me with terror. For all my love of water I never took up sailing which I now regret, and although years ago I have swum across the harbour I now no longer have the urge to take those evening dips that were my joy.

No, my Cornwall in what is now I suppose the eventide of life, is peaceful living; an awareness, a gratitude, of being allowed to end one's day in the county I fell in love with at the age of eight; to sit by a coal fire in winter evenings in a room hewn from rock listening to the water lapping outside over the slip, the same slip where I sit on summer evenings watching gulls and kingfishers. To draw my curtains in the morning and look at the beauty of Fowey harbour from my bedside, a view which never ceases to give joy. Cornwall is a county of magic. And my bit of Cornwall is the village of Bodinnick, a small slice of that magic, where a one-time boat-yard is my haven.

5

Jack Clemo

The China Clay Country

In her *Cornish Years* Anne Treneer expressed a fervent response to the ancient pagan atmosphere of West Penwith. Describing the Druidical monuments she wrote: "They speak to us in a way that Truro Cathedral cannot speak. The old stone circles and cromlechs appeal to a side of our nature which Christianity has never touched and which is nevertheless our vital selves." It was largely because of this attitude, which sometimes crept into the Cornish nationalist movement, that I refused for so many years to identify myself with Cornish culture. If Cornish loyalists are supposed to find these grim pillars, associated with blood sacrifices to the sun and moon, more congenial than Christian symbols, then I could never be a Cornish loyalist. A Penwith cromlech might prompt more sober thoughts to me than in a tourist who casually flicks a toffee-wrapping at it, but my "vital self" would not be touched any more than the tourist's. The dark, tragic Celtic spirit has always seemed foreign even to what was dark and tragic in me. I would not object to a whimsical link with King Arthur, for if he was not part of Christian history he was at least part of an innocent and romantic Christian mythology. But I could not write about him or about anything of our historical and legendary inheritance which authors like Anne Treneer and Quiller-Couch found so inspiring. My Cornwall is different, at once more starkly modern and more radically mystical.

The small bit of our county which has stamped its features on my work is an area from which all Celtic fascination has been exorcised by a voracious and apocalyptic industry. In my childhood and youth I enjoyed climbing around Roche Rock, but the oratory perched on its black schorl crags, and the range of clay-cones and flat white burrows fanning out behind it, had dissolved any " spells of the tribal night " that may once have been potent there. Much more poignant to me, and nearer to my home, was Carne Hill, which rises massively to the clay-bearing uplands from the southern fringe of Goss Moor, holding on its flanks the bleak, thickly populated village of St. Dennis. This hill is said to have been one of the last Celtic strongholds in the west of England, but I felt no contact with remote history when I saw or described it. The parish church dominated the scarp, and further down the slope, in a farmhouse by Enniscaven, I was first stirred as a poet, driven inward to shape my own creative history, when I met a preacher's daughter there at the age of thirteen. Later, in my twenties, the whole scene around St. Dennis, especially the long gnarled ridge of Rostowrack (now almost buried under rubble but then flat and open except for two dumps on each side of the road) became even more incisive and stimulating to me. The episode which began at the farm-house had ended ; I had found solace in a young St. Dennis girl whom I could meet only when she chose to visit me, as I was penniless and had become hard of hearing. In the evening dusk I often stumbled along the brambled paths of Rostowrack, sometimes climbing part way up a dump to get a better view of the girl's home as I breathed a prayer over my fading dream. The search for personal fulfilment, both spiritual and emotional, had grown so intense that I scarcely realised that it was taking place in Cornwall. I knew that it was taking place amongst vast white craters and mountainous gravel-heaps, among belching stacks and steaming kilns, and I knew that this scene was generally termed the Cornish china clay district. But I used the weird features simply because they were there, and not because, being a Cornishman, I felt the need to commend my native county to my readers.

The fierce, primitive isolationism that spurred me during those years was rooted partly in circumstance and partly in temperament. Both my parents came from families which had probably been prolific in Cornwall for centuries, but the elements nearest to me were in conflict. Working-class poverty dogged both, but my father's family at Trethosa were rough pagans, while my mother's family at Goonvean farm were models of Victorian piety, her father being a Methodist lay preacher. The struggle between these two forces was very strong in me — far too strong to allow me to draw sentimental and elegant pictures of Cornish life. The awareness of natural pagan darkness akin to D. H. Lawrence's, and the desperate need to get it subdued and transformed by Christianity, were so oppressive that I was cut off from almost all external interests. It was not physical handicaps that separated me from my fellows. Apart from two attacks of eye trouble in childhood I had no physical handicaps till I was nearly twenty. Neighbours wondered why I didn't get a job and enjoy social activities. The reason was psychological. I was inwardly split and tortured by religious and erotic tensions, and knowing that ordinary village folk would never comprehend this mystical strife I instinctively shunned them, shrinking away alone among the desolate crags and mounds of the clayworks, where I " fashioned an art from obscure mutiny," as I put it in my poem " The Islets," addressed to Emily Bronte:

" Given the fit frame, we would still
Be driven to covenant and vigil, naming
Clue for clue, flash for flash,
Cornish blood stung by heaven's lash."

One reason why I failed to get any of my early novels published was that I could not portray the progressive, civilised, gregarious life of the Cornish people at all. I had no inside knowledge either of normal employment or normal recreation. I had never entered a pub or a dance-hall, a secondary school or a Youth Club. I had never seen a talkie or a football match. Even in childhood my contacts with communal gaiety were very limited. My mother took me to the annual carnival at St. Stephen's, but my reactions were odd for a boy. I felt only a piercing sense of exile that made me want to cry, especially when the procession passed for the last time through the long main street (bordered on one side by the melancholy church-yard) and the strains of the band grew faint among the shadowy trees. There was usually a tableau on a lorry or farm waggon in which a group of young people played guitars or accordians as they sang " Uncle Tom Cobbleigh and all." I always found that song unbearably poignant ; I still can't understand why. The Cornish are deeply moved by music, but all the villagers who thronged the pavement beside me were laughing or grinning as the haunting tune floated away above the harlequins and fairies. Another contact with bustling traditional Cornwall left only a garish scar on my memory. This was the occasion when my uncle Horatio took me to Summercourt Fair. He meant well, of course; he wanted the fair to be part of my Cornwall, but it never could be. When he lifted me on to the roundabouts I just sat dazed and frightened, clutching the metal rail, and after the hobby-horse had been whirled around a few times I was seized with a panicky fear that it would never stop, that we would never get back to solid ground, never get home . . . The artist in me could not use such material.

I kept abreast of the main local development, but chiefly through hearing gossip or scanning the local paper. Councils, committees and boards of management were constantly planning for the modernisation of the St. Austell area and the clay industry. I accepted the results stolidly except when they produced new objects which I could use as symbols, such as excavators at the pit-heads and big flaring arc-lights on the tips at night. If I showed any public spirit I always had a private motive. Just before the second World War a scheme was afoot for the building of a school at my remote little hamlet of Goonamarris, to which senior scholars would come from the surrounding villages. I was then in the emotional phase in which schoolgirls between the ages of nine and fifteen were the only persons with whom I could share the romantic innocence that was emerging from my firmer grip on the Christian faith, and my longing for more frequent contact with a schoolgirl led me to write a letter to the local press in warm support of this educational scheme. But it was later abandoned. A more fruitful bit of committee work was the proposal to turn a disused clay-pit at Nanpean into a recreation ground, with playing fields, swings for children, seats on the verdant terraces and a footpath winding up the shaggy slope that had once been a bare blasted cliff-face slapped by hose-jets. The transformation was a skilful and valuable achievement, carried out by the villagers themselves, but though Nanpean was only a mile from my home I didn't bother to visit the site and see how the wilderness had been made to blossom for athletes. My inspiration lay elsewhere — in the derelict pits that no-one ever tried to reclaim. I could not write about breezy young extroverts on a tennis-court ; I could only write about some lonely village mystic clambering down into a silent clay-pit as the moon rose, seating himself in a gully just above the level of the flood-water, his heels dug into a gravelly socket where a sleeper had been ripped up, his eyes brooding on the reflection of the white sand peaks in the broad pale green pool. I had often done this myself, for Bloomdale pit, immediately behind Goonamarris, was closed and flooded, and had become one of my favourite haunts. I liked it because of its powerful atmosphere and aesthetic effects, and also because it had no morbid associations. Several other flooded pits and quarries around Nanpean, St. Dennis and Trethosa had been the scene of tragedy — suicide or accidental drowning. I was not drawn to such places. My Cornwall had a stern, solitary grandeur, but it was essentially wholesome, never a sinister and fatal trap.

The clay country has not witnessed any epic dramas of mass disaster like those which happen in Welsh coal-mines, or like that which once happened in Cornwall, at Levant tin-mine. Individual clay-workers are occasionally killed by blast or land-slides or by some mishap in handling machines. One man fell down the shaft of Goonvean engine-house. Another got his clothes caught in the jaws of an iron casket as it swung off from the loading-platform at West Slip stone quarry, which borders Goonvean. He was dragged for some distance up the aerial incline — a sort of tight-rope from which the casket dangled — and then crashed to the pit bed. In 1944 a worker was crushed to death on a dump just across the field from my cottage. An adjustable tip, a heavy wooden structure with swivelling rail-ends, was being hauled into position, tugged by a wire rope round a drum in the field. The rope snapped, the tip began sliding down the waggon-rails, and this man did not leap aside in time. I was moved and awed by these incidents, but it is significant that I did not describe them in fiction or poetry. I was trying to work out my own concept of tragedy and its solution on a subtler basis. In so far as my art was subjective I accepted only the kind of tragedy that could be outgrown while

I was still alive. On the objective plane I was more interested in the tragedies caused by human passion than in the mystery of accidental death.

The most lurid drama of passion that occurred in the clay district during my lifetime was the Halviggan affair of Christmas 1939. A labourer called Trudgian, returning home drunk from Nanpean pub and apparently inflamed with jealousy about a lodger, shot his wife, set fire to the cottage (an isolated one) and fled across the moors. His children ran in terror to the nearest neighbours, and special police were called out from St. Austell. All through the early hours of the morning the search went on while the glow from the blazing cottage tinged the white clay pyramids. In the cold dawn of Christmas Day Trudgian was detected, but he had brought his gun and as the police closed in on him he turned it on himself and dropped dead. I did not visit the charred ruins of the house, but my pagan streak gave me some insight into Trudgian's violence. My vision had always been elemental, and such eruptions as that at Halviggan helped me to focus it on the actual stuff of life reported in the newspapers. I knew that I could never see Cornwall, as a glamorous ideal or as a dusty treasure-house for antiquarians, and I felt that I could serve the real Cornwall all the better through being relentlessly honest about the human heart.

The war inevitably brought a slump in the clay industry, many pits being shut down or reduced to part-time production. The landscape took on a dreary and derelict appearance as abandoned dumps became overgrown with scrub, disused waggons rusted in drifts of gravel, and exposed buildings showed broken windows and holes in their roofs. These stricken works were a novel playground for scores of London evacuee children, and I myself enjoyed wandering around the lunar wastes with the girls who were billeted in my home. Our Saturday evening excursion to the fish-and-chip shop at Treviscoe was quite an adventure. On leaving the small grey cottage we first passed under the sagging bulk of Bloomdale burrow, then pushed through gorse-clumps and turned down a cart track hedged by bramble-matted slag-heaps. This track soon crossed a bridge at Goonvean railway siding with its rows of powdered kiln-sheds. We then had to skirt the edge of the vast pit and scramble along a glacier-like flank of the dump till we reached the fence of the main railway line. I would sit on the top wire of the fence while the two girls ran up the lane to the straggling end of Treviscoe village. The fantastic industrial mess absorbed me. A water-logged quarry coated with thick slime faced the railway track, and further east I could see the dark arch of a bridge dwarfed by swollen sand-mounds. There was an atmosphere of strangeness and peril that fitted the thoughts of war at the back of my mind. And then suddenly the bright feminine charm would be dominant again as the girls reappeared, the elder carrying our hot supper wrapped in news-sheets. After these girls had been recalled to London I often went with an older evacuee — the one I presented as Irma in my novel *Wilding Graft* — to Lower Goonvean tanks, where we fished with a jam-pot on a string, sometimes catching tadpoles or newts that bred in the muddy water.

It was during this period that I came nearest to being a clay-worker myself. I was still an abject failure as a writer, and it was obvious that before I could live my vision of " the bedrock of nuptial sense " I must have a reasonable income. I talked much with my mother about applying for a light job at Goonvean. I could probably have got it, as I was in fair health except for hardness of hearing, and the pit was operating with a skeleton staff, chiefly of elderly men. On Sundays, while my mother and the evacuees were at chapel, I often roamed around the works, trying to imagine what it would be like to be an employee, keeping to a timetable, obeying orders. My debates always ended in the same realisation that I was temperamentally incapable of wage-earning, of being in a team. This was very frustrating to my emotional hopes, and I soon began to show those moods of defensive beauty-loathing which made my first book of poems so repellent to nature-lovers.

A few of those poems owed something to the hours I spent rummaging about a scrap-heap under the dump where the tip-worker had been killed. It was just off the lane at the bottom of a field, a hundred yards from the barns and stable of my grandfather's old farm. The mica-tanks were on the other side of the lane, and beyond them the high granite walls of the engine-house loomed up amid a cluster of stacks. But it was the scrap heap itself that fascinated me. It consisted of a lot of heavy wheels and axles, sheets of rusty corrugated iron, pieces of rotten timber with loose nails sticking out of them, coils of tangled wire and tar-smeared rope. I would sit on a cogged wheel, take up a rope and spend the whole hour unwinding the strands. I liked the warm rough texture of the threads, and found the practice very relaxing, easing the strain of thought. I would smile whimsically as I contrasted the sleek, sophisticated ways of other Cornish writers with my own primitive habits. These experiences went to the making of my poem " Sufficiency ?":

> " Is there a flower that thrills
> Like frayed rope ? Is there grass
> That cools like gravel, and are there streams
> Which murmer, as clay-silt does, that Christ redeems ?"

Fortunately I have lived long enough to be thrilled by flowers as well as ropes, but at that stage I had a sort of mystical passion for industrial ugliness. I praised the scabs and eyesores, ignoring the graceful stretches of woodland that still survived (they have since been cut down and replaced by clay-filters) near my home.

It was an odd coincidence that Wesley and Cookworthy invaded Cornwall at almost the same time. Wesley's influence was, of course, the more important. His preaching transformed the spiritual and moral lives of thousands of brutalised peasants, and must have prevented many crimes similar to Trudgian's. Cookworthy did not cross the Tamar to spread piety, but to improve pottery. While these two men were in Cornwall, however, they both started processes which changed the material landscape. Gaunt little Methodist chapels sprang up like mushrooms in nearly every village, and the whole hill country between St. Austell and Goss Moor became scarred by small white excavations, which gradually deepened and widened, with more and more buildings at the pit-heads, until they grew into the massive china clay industry as we know it today, pulsing with electrical equipment and yet retaining its original crude menace as a volcanic and seismic disturbance.

For the first decade of my life the large and lonely Trethosa Chapel, standing where a lane forks down towards Meledor, meant far more to me than the clayworks. My mother was a

Sunday School superintendant there, and a member of the Tuesday class-meetings, at which a dozen or so village folk sang revivalist hymns and gave testimonies. These meetings were only for adult converts, but I had the feeling of " belonging " to something unusual and vital. I loved the winter evening services best, when I sat beside my mother and aunt, watching old Ned Varcoe ambling up and down the aisles, blinking owlishly above his bushy moustache as he raised the taper and lit the oil lamps. The pews would look warm and cosy in the yellow light, and they were well filled in those days. I was especially gripped by the week-night mission services when a visiting Wesley deaconess would exhort us with burning sincerity, making appeals that brought villagers weeping to the communion rail. But this sort of thing had virtually ended by the time I entered my teens. Even the Cornish were becoming embarrassed by emotional religion, and as emotional religion was essential to me as a man, and also as an artist — for Anne Treneer was right when she said that my poems showed " a fervour akin to that of the old wayside chapels " — I had to break away from a prosaic routine and remained a non-churchgoer for thirty years.

The religious aspect of my work is expressed chiefly in Cornish imagery, but its actual content is almost entirely non-Cornish. Swiss Calvinism, French Catholicism and American hot-gospel provide the main themes, blended with the varying shades of my personal mysticism. I am not a Methodist poet, though in " Beyond Trethosa Chapel " I revealed a poignant longing for the old fellowship, a longing stirred when a college girl from that chapel had a brief inclination to marry me. I have been saddened by trends in the local churches, the steady decline which has led to the closing of many rural Bethels. As I take such a firm stand for a supernatural and miraculous Christianity, I do not, like most Nonconformists, deplore the advance of the Roman Catholic Church in Cornwall, but even in Catholicism there is a liberal and humanist reaction. I have not come to a settled attitude towards organised religion in Cornwall. My novel *Wilding Graft* seemed to repudiate it, as all the characters are non-churchgoers and the hero merely reads his Bible while he squats on clay-dumps. This was my mood for some years after the war, but as my emotional adjustments matured I sloughed off my harsh rejection of churches along with my harsh rejection of natural beauty. I grew more benevolent towards all social accomplishments, and took some interest in the success of our famous Treviscoe Male Voice choir, which was a product of both the churches and the clayworks.

But this break-up of my obsession with grim industrial solitude involved an undercurrent of revolt against the Cornwall I had depicted. None of the young women who inspired me during my thirties and forties had much liking for the clay country. Two of them hated it, and this set up a conflict of loyalties which changed my perspective. On returning home from a short stay in Dorset in 1950 I wrote to my hostess: " I feel I have been confined too exclusively to these grimmer land- scapes and need to learn from the softer, tender kind." It might be asked why I hadn't learnt from the lush, sylvan scenes around the Fal, the Hayle and the Lynher. I had seen these places, but they hadn't moved me at all. The romantic human element wasn't there to link them with my poetic vision. When in 1964 a prospect of domestic bliss opened in the Lake District, I went there — and certainly with very different feelings from those of Anne Treneer. After touring the Lakes she merely recorded coldly that she had climbed Helvellyn and got wet. I did not climb Helvellyn, but I got gloriously wet in the vigorous, pelting downpours of the mountain region. I wrote emotional poems about rowans, and felt that I had always been starved of this benediction, this world of clean jagged fells and tumbling becks. But I have married a Londoner who spent much of her life on the Dorset coast, so I am still rather confused about landscapes (especially as I can no longer see them), sure only of what is true and abiding in the various symbols. It is noteworthy, however, that when my wife and I visited St. Ives, Fowey and St. Just-in-Roseland, I was able to extend the boundaries of my Cornwall as an artist. Sitting above Porthmeor beach in 1969 I could exult:

" My audacious luck
Shines crisp and golden as the beach below,
Sings in the surf and shells . . . "

This is Cornwall seen in the sunshine of my personal fulfilment instead of in the gloom of my early frustration. But the picture remains realistic: the very next line of this poem —

the opening poem of *The Echoing Tip* — switches the reader's
attention to the sufferings of Alfred Wallis in Madron work-
house. A writer who has plumbed the depths of loneliness and
inward conflict can never be shallow or facile in his portrayal
of human life and its background. The conventional Cornish
Riviera of the holiday-maker will never appear in my work, for
there will always be overtones of creed, the sense of victory
after spiritual struggle, which give even the beaches and the
bamboos a touch of parable and allegory. In the exotic little
church of St. Just-in-Roseland I comment that " My creed-cone
is hard as this pillar," and the word " cone " brings me back to
the clayworks. I have not discarded the positive symbols of my
native region ; I have simply become more sensitive to the
negative factors which are regretted by the claywork owners
themselves: the pollution of rivers and sea-shores, the wiping
out of whole farms, copses and even villages (such as Retew and
Karslake) as the search for new clay strata goes on. Pollution is
now being combated by inland dams, but this inevitably involves
the disappearance of more of those fertile haunts where I picked
blackberries in childhood. It was easy for me to be enchanted
with the clay fantasy then, for it seemed to be at a safe distance.
Bloomdale burrow was abreast of my home, but on the other
side of the road. To the west I could look down across four open
fields to the dumps of Goonvean and Trethosa, which squatted
like harmless white toads in the valley. Southwards there were
no clayworks in sight, only rural peace — Goonamarris farm with
its adjoining plantation, and the strip of downs rising to the
green dome of Foxhole Beacon. In the middle of the downs a
small earth-mound and a shallow excavation were visible —
relics of an unsuccessful probe for clay, the whole site so densely
overgrown with gorse, bramble and ferns that I did not regard
it as an industrial scar. Today nearly all the natural features I
have just mentioned are covered under rubble, workshops or
derelict machinery.

One can only speculate about the future of Cookworthy's
bit of Cornwall. If the post-war expansion continued unchecked,
with the use of present methods, the area would eventually
become an uninhabitable waste of craters, debris, dams and
processing plants. Experts have discussed alternative ways of
disposing of the existing dumps. Whatever changes may take

place in the landscape, the authentic china clay country of the past fifty years has been enshrined in art — in the paintings of Lionel Miskin, Christopher Wood and Ken Symonds, and in books by A. L. Rowse and myself. It was always as an artist, and as a modern mystic seeking industrial symbols in reaction against the older pagan romanticism, that I approached the strange display of restless white shapes on my native hills. The spiritual power I had felt at the chapel in my boyhood had seemed perfectly matched with the vibrating force that shook the little square engine-houses, roofed with corrugated iron, when they stood on ledges half-way up the flat burrows, operated by steam from boilers. Perhaps it was the blending of the chapel influence with that of the rumbling, clanking machinery which urged me in later years to put so much stress on dogma. At any rate, it was these two elements, toned by adolescent emotion, that first set me functioning in a way which finally brought me official recognition in the Gorsedd bardship.

That climax at St. Piran Round in 1970 was in some respects an irony, but a very pleasant one for us all. It was as a poet that I was accepted into the College of Bards. I had not been offered a bardship for my prose books twenty years earlier, as they were written soon after Cornish villagers had tried to break up my attachment to a London evacuee, and the general atmosphere of suspicion and misunderstanding had made me depict Cornish village life with a passionate realism that was not welcomed. But by 1970 I had married and mellowed, and the Cornish flavour in my poetry was that of landscape and imagery, with no comment on village gossips and bad-tempered house-wives. As my wife led me across the bumpy ground near Perranporth for the initiation, I did not feel like a returning prodigal. In one sense I had never been a prodigal son of Cornwall, and in another sense I was still as much " apart " as ever. My wife was allowed to " crown " me with the bardic hood, and though this was only permitted because of my blindness I thought it beautifully symbolic, as I am the only Cornish writer whose main theme involves a sacramental interpretation of marriage.

I had visited Perranporth several times, the first occasion being in 1934 when I was included in a family outing and my St. Dennis inspirer, then a very young girl, accompanied us. I still felt near to the clay, as my cousin, who took us in his car, was one of the last drivers of the old wooden clay-waggons, drawn by teams of horses, that creaked and lurched along the lanes to Par or Charlestown until the early 1930's. And when we got back to Goonamarris after our beach trip I wrote some verses, printed in the *Cornish Guardian,* about my "love-thought" lingering among the rocks —

> " Aloof grim sentinels,
> Sea-battered when the in-tide swells,
> Arched, twisted — beauty wild and weird . . . "

Apart from the references to tides, this might have been a description of the crags I had so often seen standing boldly out of the flood-waters in abandoned clay-pits. Anything that mirrored the clay world was congenial to me and could be fused with my romantic vision. In later years this vision inspired me even when detached from clay and Cornwall, but as my wife and I travelled home on Gorsedd day I could feel that my grasp of the essential Cornwall had been fairly wide and potent despite my inability to record its ancient history or modern social life.

6

Denys Val Baker

Cornwall seen from the Sea

" This is a hideous and wicked country
Sloping to hateful sunsets and the end of time,
Hollow with mine shafts, naked with granite, fanatic
With sorrow . . . "

Some years ago the poet John Heath-Stubbs, then living in
a coastguard cottage at Gurnard's Head, near Zennor, wrote
those passionate lines to express a profound feeling of unease :
and a similar reaction prompted the novelist, Ruth Manning-
Sanders, after a twilight walk along the Land's End cliffs, to
recall " the sense of the primordial, the strange and the savage,
the unknown, the very long ago, filling the dusk with something
that is akin to dread. It is then the place becomes haunted, a
giant heaves grey limbs from his granite bed, a witch sits in that
stone chair on the cliff."

For many years these comments remained vividly in my
mind as capturing something of the mystery that is Cornwall:
and then something happened to me which rendered them twice
as vivid, many times more profound. Early in the 1960's, thanks
to an unexpected inheritance, my wife and I were able to turn
our lifelong dream into reality and acquire a boat — a large,
strong, seagoing boat of the MFV type, as is often found in
Cornish harbours such as Newlyn, Looe and Mevagissey. That
boat is called *Sanu* and in her, over a period of nearly ten years,

we have travelled many seas, voyaging to Denmark and Sweden in the North, Spain in the South. I have written about some of these experiences in *To Sea with Sanu* — but, curiously I have hardly ever before written about our sea experiences of Cornwall.

Two " firsts " come immediately to mind, like extracts from a cine film: the one by daylight, the other a night time trauma. When we bought *Sanu* she was lying at a berth in the River Hamble, near Southampton, and so a party of five of us travelled up by train in order to bring our new acquisition down to Cornwall. It was blustery, boisterous weather, but fortunately we had with us an experienced ex-sea captain who guided us safely across Lyme Bay and around Start Point and then towards a sudden edifice rising mysteriously out of nowhere — the Eddystone Lighthouse. We knew that at last we were approaching the Cornish coast, but there was a sea mist hanging around which obliterated everything, and for some time we felt uneasily lost . . And then at last, together with an accompanying blaze of sunshine, we emerged from the mist — and there was Cornwall spread out in a vast jewelled sweep all around: Looe, Polperro, Fowey, St. Austell Bay, the dreaded Dodman Head, Portscatho, St. Anthony Head with its black and white lighthouse, the hump of Pendennis Castle, Helford and the vague outline of the Manacles — and on the horizon, like a stabbing, warning finger, the famed Lizard Point. It was all wild and beautiful and encompassing, and we gloried in the magic of it all as we steamed past Black Rock and into one of the world's largest, safest and surely most beautiful natural harbour and picked up our waiting mooring close by the Prince of Wales Pier.

That was our daytime introduction to the Cornish coast from the sea. Our night time initiation was far more alarming. We were at the end of our first cross Channel cruise (a visit to Guernsey and Jersey) and had left Gorey, Jersey, shortly after dawn on a 24 hour trip to Newlyn. All day the conditions had been pretty uncomfortable and though from time to time a brave spirit ventured below to make a cup of tea or some soup, in general we had not felt hungry. As the day darkened we tended to huddle together in the wheelhouse, contemplating a little dubiously the orange gold sky ahead of us. It was indeed a weird sort of sunset in the western sky, and I remember becoming confused by the extraordinary sequence of colour patterns — first a deep orange, then (as small clouds moved over the dying rays) a mirage of dozens of small islands. Not long after the illuminated clouds amalgamated to form an outline of cliffs so realistic that I kept saying hopefully: " Perhaps we've come faster than we realised and we can actually see the Lizard?" Alas, a quick look at the Walker log unfolding at the stern proved this to be an impossibility.

In fact it was another three or four hours before the now pitch black sky ahead of us was broken for the first time by the three quick flashes of the Lizard lighthouse. I think we all gave a small cheer then, for this meant we were well on course. Here came an important lesson in night travel at sea — it's likely to be a long way between seeing and finding. I don't mean we were in any doubt about the general whereabouts of the Lizard. What bothered — and more so as I was very tired, having been at the wheel without a break for some fifteen hours — was the difficulty I had in estimating just how near we were to the lighthouse itself (this was, of course, my first experience of navigation by night). Sometimes as I stared ahead desperately trying to pierce the darkness it seemed as if we were almost on top of the Lizard. Once indeed, through some kind of momentary hallucination, I even became convinced I could see the clifftop around the light-house and the actual shape of houses — whereas someone pointed out after a check on the Walker log, and the time, that we were still at least 20 miles away! Intellectually I agreed, but emotionally I remained disturbed, being haunted by a daytime memory of passing the Lizard and seeing all those angry rocks: supposing we came upon them before I could steer clear? Haunted by this horrifying vision I finally gave in to my fears and played safe by steering a more westerly course . . . Of course the result was a minor disaster: we quickly became really off course: the Lizard kept appearing in different positions so that it became difficult to estimate which way we should be heading.

At last we managed to get back on course, but our troubles were not over, by any means. It was still very dark and there would be no more lighthouses, only the entrance lights of Penzance and Newlyn harbours. And where exactly were they?

I peered with sore eyes to right and left, matters not being helped by the arrival of a faint drizzle. By now not only I but the other members of our party were understandably edgy ; we differed volubly about what course to follow or what the various distant lights portended. From that blessed nautical bible, Reeds Almanac, we had verified that Newlyn Pier flashed every five seconds — and, look, there it was, flashing away! I steered grimly for that last objective, but by now tiredness was sweeping over me in great waves: I found that I was seeing lights and shapes that weren't there, and I had grave doubts as to whether I should ever manage to bring my boat safely into harbour. Thank goodness I had companions to sustain my spirits ; and thanks to them, at long weary last, just as a cold grey light of another dawn was falling on the sea behind us, I steered *Sanu* through the narrow neck of Newlyn Harbour and up to the nearest vacant patch of quayside. Five minutes later and we could have made a more comfortable entry by daylight — a lesson I have never forgotten!

Since then our experiences of Cornwall from the sea have been as differing as those two initial episodes: and perhaps indeed, on reflection, this pattern is typical of Cornwall as a whole? Many times we have been in *Sanu* sailing down some lovely stretch of coastline, the sea calm as the proverbial mirror, the wind non-existent, the sun shining — imagine, in such tranquil conditions, making a trip that became quite familiar to us, from Newlyn Harbour out round St. Catherine's Isle and down past the savage grandeur of the heather strewn cliffs around Lamorna Cove and Penberth and the new light at Tater Du, past the glorious white sloping sands of Porthcurno and the outline of Minack Theatre, finally rounding the mournful Runnelstone Whistle Buoy (close to Porthgwarra with its ominously placed " storm cones," fortunately on such a day not set up) and then coming to that most romantic of all sights, the Longships Lighthouse, with all the rugged cliffs of Land's End (and that ugly hotel) forming a majestic background — on and on, past England's only cape, Cape Cornwall, steering well clear of the menacing Brissons, and then, taking a bearing on Pendeen Lighthouse and Botallack's crumbling mine stacks, heading eastwards up the North Cornish Coast, past the lovely cliff scenery of Gurnard's Head and Zennor — finally rounding the last point of Clodgy and suddenly entering the beautiful sweep of St. Ives Bay, perhaps (if the tide is still out of the harbour) joining at anchor some of the glorious red and white and blue crabbers over from Audierne in Britanny . . .

Yes, on such a day Cornwall from the sea is very Heaven. And yet the coin can well and truly be reversed, and in exactly the same setting . . . I can well remember a time when we set out gaily with a party of friends (" come for the trip ") only to encounter really rough weather so that once we reached Land's End and Cape Cornwall we were taking huge waves on our beam ; with every wave *Sanu* was lifted up and turned half way round, and then down again with a sinking feeling. One by one our guests began to turn pale: there was little appreciation of those wonderful scenic beauties! Rounding Clodgy we had an alarming view of Porthmeor, great white breakers rolling up to the sea wall. When we rounded the Island and came in sight of that patch of the bay where French crabbers usually lay peacefully at anchor — there was only one solitary boat, being tossed about wildly in the rough sea. It was too rough to enter the harbour, and we had to anchor and spend a miserable night, pacing up and down deck wondering if our CQR anchor would hold or whether we would be dragged on to the rocks by Porthminster.

Perhaps not surprisingly, many of our more nerve-racking sea experiences have taken place around Land's End. Once, when setting off on a long summer cruise that was to take us across the Channel to Le Havre and then 250 miles up the River Seine to the very centre of Paris, we had our most alarming experience of the whole trip rounding Land's End (from St. Ives) in a fairly rough sea. *Sanu* was being thrown around quite strenuously, and we were just level with the Longships Lighthouse (rather too near, really) when — sudden, terrifying silence. The main engine had stopped! Fortunately we had had a small side engine installed as a precaution against just such a happening, and two of us rushed down and started this, and we were able to manoeuvre away from those uncomfortably close and very jagged sea-washed rocks . . . We then discovered that the rough sea movement had sent an oil drum toppling and it had accidentally turned off the fuel tap to the main engine! On another occasion, returning from a visit to Cork in Ireland, our overnight passage had ended in the reassuring triumph of seeing the lights of Round House, and of Pendeen and indeed of Longships ahead. Alas, between then and the rising of dawn, thick fog descended and we were suddenly, alarmingly, lost — knowing that we were within a mile or so of all those relentless rocks . . . by great good fortune the fog finally cleared in time for us to identify Najizel Bay.

In many ways Land's End, and the Penwith peninsula in general, typifies the romantic Cornwall which is certainly visible in plentiful quantities from the sea. But other parts of the Cornish coast can be just as beautiful — and indeed just as forbidding and even menacing. Around the Lizard, for instance: I am never so relieved as when our boat has finally rounded that squat seemingly endless point, with all its dangerous off lying rocks. Or Dodman Head, with its solitary cross on top of the cliffs — there is something about its bleak, brooding shape which would strike unease into the most sensitive soul. Gribben Head, by Fowey, I find more cheerful somehow, perhaps because it marks the entry to our home port! Mind you, Cornwall has little to offer in the way of shelter, really — only Fowey, with its river wandering up to Golant and Lostwithiel, and Falmouth, with its much larger river mouth and estuary, offer any real sense of security to the boat owner. Still, we must be thankful for small mercies, and both ports have much to offer. There is much to be said, as we have so often done in the past, for sailing past St. Anthony Head Lighthouse and suddenly being out of all sea way and feeling a sense of balm and peace . . . taking up a mooring among dozens of other exciting looking craft, mid way between Falmouth and Flushing — and then turning off the engine and relaxing, just relaxing. Bliss, perfect bliss, to sit back and watch some old trading schooner fluttering red sails in the breeze, or a tug boat manoeuvring in some large ocean-going cargo ship, or some sleek racing yacht rounding a buoy — or even the friendly old St. Mawes ferry chugging by. Harbours the world over are, literally, havens, friendly and fascinating places — and here Cornwall has much to offer. Falmouth and Fowey are the most sheltered ; but many others are of great interest: Newlyn, centre of a working fishing industry, Looe and Mevagissey, very similar, or smaller ports which still mix business and pleasure, like Polperro, Coverack, Cadgwith or, round on the other coast St. Ives, Newquay, Padstow and Bude.

One of the most interesting experiences of Cornwall from the sea is to do what we often did, and enter a land-locked port of the old kind, such as Hayle. A sand bar confines entry to Hayle to around the high tide mark, but once across it is a fascinating little port, full of historical reminders of a golden heyday. Porthleven is another such port, though we have never actually entered there — in many ways, from all accounts thanks to its flourishing boatyard business, Porthleven appears to be enjoying quite a revival. Another port which we have, to be frank, never dared to enter, but which is an absolute gem, is Polperro. Like Mousehole it has lock gates to close it off from the worst of winter storms. A port which we once literally entered with a bang is Mevagissey: it was the subject of our very first nervous local " trip," and owing to inexperience in reversing in time our bow struck the outer wall a resounding wallop, fortunately with no real damage either way. We were able to recover from our momentary shock and climb up on the quay and have an inquisitive walk around our first " official " port of call. Cornwall's ports are really very diversified and full of interest ; and usually they represent triumphs of manpower over the elements, having often been hewn out of granite surrounds, or artificially built up to withstand big seas (not always successfully, as Mevagissey and Portmellon discovered).

Personally I have always found ports to represent the most congenial aspects of cruising in boats, and Cornish ports are no exception. They are full of unexpected character — just, I suppose, as are the Cornish people themselves. I love it when *Sanu* is berthed at Newlyn, probably alongside one of the Stevenson trawlers, or maybe some visitor from Belgium, and the air is full of the smell of tar and fishing nets, and fishermen's talk. Newlyn is very much a working port, with its rows of working boats, the coming and going of fish lorries, the market place — but in addition it has a quaint architectural beauty of its own, the little huddled cottages climbing up the hills — and several snug pubs, too, like the Star and the Dolphin and the Tolcarne. In a sizeable port like Newlyn — or Mevagissey or Looe — one encounters a man-made world of boats and machinery and equipment. In some of the much smaller Cornish ports — places, for instance, like Cadgwith on the Lizard, or Portloe on Roseland, or miniature places like Penberth and Porthgwarra, with just a few dinghies pulled up on the granite slipway, here one enters an altogether more romantic world, peopled by a sturdy lot of individuals who somehow eke a living with just a small boat and a few lobster pots or crab pots. It often seems to me that these smaller places mirror some of the qualities of the coastal world of Cornwall generally — everything is more strongly defined, very individualistic. One thing nobody could be in doubt about, either regarding the Cornish coastline or the Cornish people — there is no mistaking them! As one who, from his own boat, has seen the white cliffs of Dover, the flat sand ridges of Holland, the islands of Denmark, the coasts of Sweden, Germany, France and Spain, I can truthfully say that while all have their favourable aspects, not one of them could possibly be mistaken for the familiar Cornish outlines. Or perhaps one other coast can be compared — and that is of Britanny, a fellow Celtic land. In Britanny, sailing off the Chausse de Seine, or Belle Isle, we have often found ourselves comparing the rocks and cliffs with Cornwall.

And what about that "hideous and wicked country sloping to hateful sunsets and the end of time?" Well, it is all very much there, when you look in from the sea. Often on our voyages we take *Sanu* quite close in to the coast, and this gives an interesting impression not only of the sea washed ragged rocky edges — but of further inland. Along the North Coast between St. Ives and Cape Cornwall, for instance, part of the total effect is the rearing hills and moorlands rising up away from the coast, capped as like as not by some weird and mysterious carn or quoit. The same thing is applicable to the approach across Mount's Bay, with the line of Penwith hills — capped by Trencrom, from which giants of old used to toss quoits into the sea — making a panoramic background.

There is, in short, always a sense of mystery about what we might call the Cornish seascape. This was very much epitomised for me once when we were crossing Mount's Bay from the Lizard in extremely rough and misty conditions. For a long time we could not see land at all, and yet were uneasily conscious of the strong winds setting us too far into the bay, so that at any moment we feared to find ourselves almost on top of Porthleven, or the nearby strange Looe Pool. Suddenly, as the wind blew stronger, the mist began to disperse — and there ahead of us, indeed very much on our wrong side, we saw the weird outline of St. Michael's Mount, rising up sheerly out of the sea. There was a tiny sailing yacht battling against the wind to clear the Mount, and we watched enthralled as it was flung about by the rough seas — while ourselves taking good care to get back on the sea side of the Mount (they say you can sail between the Mount and the mainland at some stages of the tide, but I wouldn't like to try it, especially in a rough sea!). It was all a most dramatic setting, and very Cornish.

Cornwall from the sea, of course, would not be complete without a word or two about that very most western extremity — The Isles of Scilly. During our early years with *Sanu* we gravitated many times to the delectable Duchy. To this day I do not know anything quite to compare with the sheer excitement of looking out from *Sanu's* wheelhouse and seeing the first appearance of those misty humps of land on the horizon. We used to arrange our arrival at St. Mary's for about nine o'clock of a summer evening, just nice time to tie up at the quay and have a last round of drinks at the famous Mermaid pub. After a day or two of "civilisation" at Hughtown, we would start *Sanu's* old Kelvin and motor over to Tresco, picking our way carefully by the large scale chart through Tresco Flats, and finally anchoring just off New Grimsby Quay, not far from Commander Dorrien Smith's cutter. We would spend idyllic sunny days there, just a few oars' strokes either from Tresco's tropical beauty, or the lush vegetation and wild cliffs of Bryher. For anyone with a boat, of course, the Scillies are an endless paradise, full of elemental beauty and a sense of history. And of course with a smaller boat — we had a tough old Zodiac inflatable — it is easy to visit many of the smaller offshore islands, like Samson and Gugh, St. Agnes and St. Martin's.

All these things we used to do, and we thought we knew the Scillies quite well . . . but the time came for the inevitable Cornish turn of the coin. One night we anchored off Cromwell Castle, Tresco, just below Hangman's Isle (we should have taken warning from such a name!), and just before dusk, slipped ashore in the dinghy for a last drink at the New Inn. *Sanu* had been at anchor for five or six hours without stirring, and all seemed well. Alas, all was not well . . . when we returned in the dinghy *Sanu's* bright anchor light was not in the same position as when we had left — it was far too much over to starboard — so much so that the outline of Cromwell Castle was, unbelievably, on the seaward side of *Sanu*!

"She's aground!" I cried out in anguish. "She's on the rocks!"

She was, too — high and dry on the rocks, and heeling over at an alarming angle, the lower deck still awash with water from a tide which was almost at its lowest, leaving about four feet around the hull.

Later, after I had called the lifeboat from St. Mary's, on the telephone in the village, we all gathered, a bedraggled collection, in the shelter of Cromwell Castle, and waited. When we saw the distant light of the lifeboat winking in the darkness we somehow managed to clamber out upon *Sanu* to try and help. After a spot of difficult manoeuvring the lifeboat came alongside and landed a yellow oil-skinned crew member to assess the situation. His decisive comment was not reassuring, though very much to the point: "She'm as full as an egg!" he cried out.

There was nothing, it appeared that could possibly be done for the moment, for the boat was not only heeled over but full of water, and would never right of her own accord. Something might be attempted at the next high tide — meantime we were ordered to allow ourselves to be removed to safety by the life-boat. Once aboard, we were treated most kindly: out came the inevitable self heating cans of soup, of which I had often read, but hardly expected to see under such circumstances. Then we headed for St. Mary's. So far things had carried the overtones of a dream, or rather a nightmare, but when we now heard the radio operator ringing through for a representative of the Ship-wrecked Mariners Association to meet us, we began to realise how grimly real our situation was. Sure enough there was a kind official to meet us — although it was a Sunday morning he had already arranged for a local cafe to open up to serve us with a welcome hot breakfast. Nor was this all. While we ate, our new counsellor made a quick list of essential clothing needed, for all ours were under water — and in half an hour was back bearing precious bundles. When I add that during the same early period of the morning he also found billets for us for the ensuing night, then perhaps I convey some idea of the essentially down to earth practical help we received from an organisation which recognises no differences or barriers — to them a shipwrecked mariner, whether master or mate, crew or passenger, is just that: someone suddenly in serious trouble, most likely shocked and certainly distressed and needing immediate sustenance.

Our experience on the Scillies ended more happily with *Sanu* being salvaged and eventually towed over to Falmouth for complete repairs — but needless to say the traumatic overtones linger to this day. It is, I often feel, a little unfair that people remember a single disaster so easily, and overlook the fact that we have cruised many thousands of miles all over the North West hemisphere! On the other hand, it is probably a good thing that, in our dealings with Cornwall from the sea (just as I might suggest, at the risk of repetition, might apply in dealings with Cornwall from any angle!) we have been taught such a severe lesson. Now when I look upon some majestic rearing cliff, falling down to some delightfully picturesque cove — or see the long white line of some surfing beach, or the humped shapes of distant mysterious islets — I remain just a little more on guard than might otherwise have been the case. I know that nine times out of ten, the sun will shine, the sea will glisten a quiet blue, and the winds will be fragrant and weak . . . but I also know that, inevitably, there will be the tenth time, when all is changed. If you have ever stood on some lonely Cornish shore or on one of the big beaches like Porthmeor or Newquay or Perranporth and watched huge waves pounding in under some near gale force wind — then I wouldn't mind wagering you have been touched by two predominant emotions. First, you have marvelled at the stark and terrible beauty of it all — and secondly, I have no doubt, you have spared a thought for those poor unfortunates who might be somewhere "out there," enduring all that rough sea.

Well, quite often, aboard *Sanu*, we have indeed been "out there" in some such stormy seas — probably, in fact, not at all as far " out there " as we would have liked, for in bad weather the more sea room the better. At such times the close proximity of all those rugged cliffs, those craggy rocks, those evil looking under water obstructions — is neither romantic or mysterious or edifying in any way — they are simply quite terrifying. Under such conditions, with white crested waves cascading high in the air as they break on distant rocks — with great rollers roaring up some not distant enough white sandy beach — with spray often clouding the very top of cliffs — one would give almost anything in the world to be a thousand miles away from the cursed Cornish coastline!

But then, a day later, the scene has changed again. The sun shines, the sea sparkles, the boat glides gently along, on yet another fascinating pilgrimage along one of the most intricate, the most mysterious, and the most beautiful coastlines in the whole wide world. And if, as dusk falls, one is inclined to remember Mrs. Manning Sanders' wise words — " It is then the place becomes haunted, a giant heaves grey limbs from his granite bed, a witch sits in that stone chair on the cliff " — well, isn't that really what makes Cornwall so rare and wonderful and magical a place ?

7

Colin Wilson

Gorran

In the summer of 1954, I was 'sleeping rough' in London — mostly on Hampstead Heath, and spending my days in the British Museum reading room, writing my first novel, *Ritual in the Dark*. Possibly this sounds romantic; in fact, it was pretty wearing to the nerves. And in mid-July, when my girlfriend Joy (now my wife) got a fortnight's holiday from the library where she worked, my one thought was to get as far out of London as possible. Neither of us had been to Cornwall. So we sent our bikes on to Plymouth by rail, and set out to hitch-hike from London. We stuck to the coast road — Southampton, Poole, Bridport — and I remember that it was in Lyme Regis, climbing that steep hill out of the town, looking at the seagulls nesting on the cliffs, that the weight of oppression suddenly slipped from my shoulders, and I experienced a sense of 'newness,' sheer delight.

I should explain that I am a Midlander; I was born in Leicester, and spent most of my life there until I moved to London at twenty. But I am no lover of industrial landscape, or provincial towns. During my teens, I spent a great deal of time cycling around Leicestershire, Warwickshire, Derbyshire. I had even cycled to the Lake District. But none of this quite prepared me for the West country. I had seen pictures of Devon and Cornwall fishing villages : but they had seemed as remote as

Hong Kong or Tahiti. I suppose what astonished me, and shook me into wakefulness, was their accessibility. It seemed amazing that you could get there so easily, without even the train fare in your pocket. I kept thinking: Why didn't I do this before? At seventeen, you suspect that life is going to be an endless series of obstacles and difficulties. The problem of a career — of how you are going to make a living for the next sixty years or so — hangs over you like some symbolic taskmaster with a whip. And it seems that the possibilities you dreamed about in childhood — travel, adventure, fame — are as remote from real life as a Walt Disney movie. I was inclined to agree with Axel, who calls the world ' an old slave . . who promises us the keys to a palace of enchantment, when it clutches only a handful of ashes in its clenched black fist.' So when I first saw the West Country, I was inclined to be suspicious, believing that there must be a catch in it somewhere.

We sat on the quay at Paignton, and ate bananas with Devon cream, and looked at the boats in the harbour, and the fishermen who were obviously real, and not made-up for a pantomime ; and again I experienced the sense of freedom, and the suspicion that there had to be a catch in it somewhere. There was ; the bananas and cream made me feel sick ; but that didn't last long, and the scenery was still there when it passed away.

We drank cider in a pub, and had our water bottles filled up with it. The landlord said in a friendly manner: ' Ah, that'll rot your socks off.' It didn't quite do that ; but it acquired a most peculiar tang from the metal of the army water bottles, and tasted like paint-thinners when we tried to drink it for breakfast the next morning. We poured it on the stiff, blue-green grass at the edge of Dartmoor, and I swear it had begun to wilt when we left an hour later . .

Joy had a pocket-size copy of Arthur Norway's Highways and Byeways in Devon and Cornwall, and we took turns to reading it aloud. The style is somewhat flowery: ' To all west countrymen (Exeter) is a mother city, one who during untold centuries has been their head and capital, and fought their battles and suffered with them when the luck was bad.' In London I would have been very sniffy about this kind of prose ; my ideal was the unemotional precision of Eliot, the flat statement of Hemingway. How the hell could a city fight your battles and suffer with you? But in the West country, it became part of the enchantment ; I could understand why this particular volume of the ' Highways and Byeways ' series has more myths and fairy tales than any other.

I apologise if this sounds self-indulgently nostalgic. The experience of freedom, of widening horizons, makes an impression that lasts a lifetime, and I would be untrue to the experience if I merely described our itinerary.

In Plymouth, we collected the bikes and some camping equipment, and the going became heavier. If I had known about the steepness of West country hills, I would have brought rubber soled shoes ; the steel studded things I was wearing kept slipping backwards as I pushed the overloaded bicycle up one-in-four gradients, and Joy complained that my language spoilt the scenery. It was definitely a mistake to bring bicycles. But in the evenings, when we had set up the tent, and unloaded the primus stove and cooking pots, it was a delight to freewheel down steep hills, with the odd sensation that the bicycles had become weightless and were about to take off like aeroplanes.

What do I remember clearly about that holiday? Since I am being nostalgic, I may as well try to set it down. I remember camping above Looe, and going to see a film called (I think) ' The Knave of Hearts ' in a kind of hall in Polperro. This was before the death of Gerard Philippe, and I remember being amazed by his sheer lightness of touch, a champagne-like quality in the comedy that reinforced the mood of the holiday. (His death struck me as a greater tragedy than that of James Dean or Marilyn Monroe). I remember camping in a field near Gorran churchtown, only a few hundred yards from where we now live, and cycling down to Mevagissey thinking that the main square, with its lighted shops, looked exactly like a stage set — and a particularly unreal one at that. The next morning the heat of the sun exploded the front tyre on my bike, but I was able to buy a replacement at Ernie Liddicoat's garage on the corner, although it seemed a pity to waste money on this kind of thing when it could be spent on fish and chips and cider. (By this time I had acquired a taste for the vinegary Devon cider, and was upset to find that most of the Cornish pubs stocked only the bottled variety). I remember the exhilaration of the stiff breeze on the St. Mawes seafront, and of travelling over to Falmouth on the ferry, watching the sunlight on the choppy water. I remember walking too close to a rough sea at St. Ives, and getting soaked from head to foot by a large wave, and then running, shivering, back to the camp on the cliff to change. I also recall being disappointed by Hell's Mouth, which didn't strike me as nearly spectacular enough after all the other Cornish cliffs.

What impressed me most about Cornwall ? The jagged rocks in the sea, and the pleasantness of its pubs. After living in a town all my life, the sheer quantity of fine scenery seemed excessive. And having got used to town pubs, with their large rooms and juke boxes and tarted-up decorations, it was delightful to enter small bars where you had to stoop to avoid the beams, and where it all looked as dark and old as if it hadn't changed in two centuries.

But most important, I suppose: that the trip occurred when it did: at a time when I'd determined to become a writer or bust. If it had happened six years earlier, when I was seventeen, and working in Leicester at the Collector of Taxes, it would only have filled me with an awful nostalgia and dissatisfaction, and become a symbol of all the things I was missing. But it happened when I had already decided that I'd had enough of conventional existence and ' playing it safe ' — when I'd determined that I'd rather become a tramp or a monk than spend my life doing an ordinary job. I felt I'd cut my cables, and there was no return. (I even remember telling Joy, as we cycled through Par, that she shouldn't regard our relationship as too permanent, because one day I'd probably end in a monastery). And Cornwall seemed like a kind of advance payment of freedom, a confirmation of the decision to cut loose.

Subsequent visits reinforced this mood. We returned the following year, this time without bicycles. Since my last trip, I had moved indoors again — to a room in New Cross — and written most of a book called *The Outsider*. Some time around March, 1955, I had submitted a dozen or so pages of this book to a publisher, Victor Gollancz, and he replied almost immediately that he would be interested in publishing it. Shortly before we set out for Cornwall, I had sent Gollancz about half

71

the typescript. He had replied that he would definitely publish it, and took me out to lunch. When we took a holiday in Cornwall, I still had one chapter to write, and I had that excited, slightly sick feeling that children get on Christmas Eve. Now the book would definitely be published, I could at last think in terms of a career — a real career ; the next stage was to finish my novel *Ritual in the Dark* and then write a sequel to *The Outsider* about religious mystics. The butterflies-in-the-stomach feeling sprang out of a sort of fear: the feeling that I had so much to say, so much work ahead of me . . . and that there could still be a slip ' between cup and the lip.' Perhaps Gollancz wouldn't like the second half of the book, and would decide not to publish after all . . . But drinking again in the low-beamed Cornish pubs, and scrambling across rocks at the edge of the sea, I couldn't really believe anything would go wrong.

I was correct. My assumption of the immediate fame that would follow publication was sheer inexperience, but it happened. *The Outsider* came out (in May, 1956) at a time when the literary scene had been quiescent for a year or so. Dylan Thomas had died three years earlier, and his death had seemed to mark the end of the ' apocalyptic ' era — of Isherwood's Berlin novels and the poems of Auden and Spender, and Ronald Duncan's *This Way to the Tomb*. And although a few new talents had appeared in the early fifties — Amis, Wain, Iris Murdoch, Angus Wilson — there was still no sign of a 'generation,' a group of writers with a general direction. I suppose *The Outsider*, and Osborne's *Look Back in Anger* (which appeared earlier the same month) appeared to be ' landmarks,' in the same sense as *The Waste Land* or *Ulysses*. (I certainly thought of *The Outsider* as my own *Waste Land*). Whatever the reason, I had more than a successful book on my hands ; I also had a reputation as some sort of figurehead of a new generation. For a few months it looked as if Osborne and myself had achieved, in one single step, the kind of dominant position that other writers had only achieved after several books.

So when Joy and I returned to the West Country in July, 1956, we were in a different position from in previous years. To begin with, there was enough money to eat restaurant meals, and also enough to take ourselves — and our bikes — on trains when we got tired of pedalling. This time we drove down to Devon in style, sharing a sports car (or at least, the cost of the petrol) with Ken Allsop and Dan Farson. We stayed for a couple of days with Dan's father, Negley — author of *Way of a Transgressor* — and met Henry Williamson, and Negley's next door neighbour Malcolm Elwin (whose *First Romantics* was one of my favourite books). All this was a little breath-taking — to mix with authors, to be praised by critics, to be written about in magazines and newspapers. I didn't entirely like it. I'm a retiring sort of person, basically rather shy. Being approved of so much was a strain, like walking on a tightrope. I would have been happier if the book had simply made me a reputation as an ' interesting ' writer, worth watching. For an introvert, the best-seller status was unnerving. I felt like that little soldier in Akutagawa's Yam Gruel, who always dreams of being able to eat his fill of yam gruel — until a rich samurai with a sense of humour invites him to his home, and then places vast turreens of yam gruel in front of him. (Naturally, he just feels sick).

So this time, the West Country was simply a tonic for the nerves, and I can remember nothing about that trip, except that the porter failed to unload our bikes at the Launceston railway station, and we had to spend the night camping in a nearby field, waiting for them to be sent back from Penzance . . .

And that might well have been the end of my relationship with the West country — except for the occasional holidays — if it had not been for chance. My mistrust of the overnight fame proved justified. As the success rolled on like some giant snow-ball, and *The Outsider* went through impression after impression, people naturally began to ask if I was really all that brilliant and original, and if I deserved quite so much publicity and praise. England's ' intellectual establishment ' felt they had been stampeded, and people who had never joined in the praise took the opportunity to say they'd never considered the book much good anyway. By Christmas, it seemed that every critic in England was willing to admit that the whole thing had been an absurd mistake. I was utterly and totally ' discredited,' as if I'd been a confidence swindler who had been publicly exposed. There was still plenty of publicity, but now it was uniformly hostile. Victor Gollancz, who had sold 40,000 copies of the book — as well as selling it to America and a dozen foreign publishers — saw his investment dwindling. He advised me to take a job and spend five years writing my next book. When I showed no sign of accepting this advice, he suggested that I move to a cottage in the country, and try to keep out of the newspapers. Early in 1957, sick of the atmosphere of hostility in London, I decided to try out his suggestion. I rented a room in a huge old house near Totnes, belonging to Hugh Heckstall Smith, a retired headmaster; but it was lonely without Joy. I returned to London, and more publicity. A poet living in the same house (in Notting Hill Gate) asked me if I'd be interested in renting his cottage near Mevagissey. One weekend in early March, we travelled down by train, and spent the evening at a guest house owned by D. S. Savage, the literary critic, in Mevagissey. The next morning a taxi drove us out through Portmellon, up the incredibly steep hill that we had freewheeled down three years earlier (Bodrugan) and on to the farm at the top of the hill. Down a long, muddy track, we found the cottage, with white cob walls that were nearly a yard thick, and a corrugated tin roof painted blue. It had four rooms — two up and two down — and a bathroom with an ancient boiler. If you stood in the bedrooms, you could see the rooms below through cracks in the floorboards. There was no electricity — it was too far off the main road — and drinking water came from a well in the garden. The cottage was in the bottom of a green valley, which led down to the sea. A noisy stream flowed near the front door, so that it always sounded as if it were raining heavily. And there were even some flowers growing on the trellis around the door although (not being much of a countryman) I can't recall what they were. The rent was thirty shillings a week, which was also a consideration — I had already spent most of the royalties from *The Outsider*. We decided immediately to take it, on a two year lease. A couple of weeks later, we hired a van, packed all our belongings in it, and drove down from London.

It ought to have been idyllic — the country existence. The spring that year was superb. The scenery was magnificent for walking; the great cliffs between Portmellon and Gorran Haven, with the isolated beach at Chapel Point. We bought an old car — for £40 — so Mevagissey became easily accessible. When this contraption exploded after a few months, we bought a new Anglia, and started to explore Cornwall. I certainly had no regrets about leaving London and the 'literary scene,' with its empty headedness and bitchery. But the experience of the past year had been too vertiginous, and I was suffering from a kind of moral hangover. Three years earlier, I had been in Mevagissey, dreaming about literary fame. Now it had arrived — and gone. So the quiet had an ominous quality, as if this were the place where I had been left by a receding tide.

Fortunately, I am a recluse by nature. At Old Walls, I finished my second book. *Religion and the Rebel,* and it appeared later that year. Predictably, the critics found in it all the shortcomings they had subsequently discovered in *The Outsider ;* everyone seemed to experience a great relief at being able to declare that this book was unadulterated rubbish.' By then, I had been taking abuse for so long that it seemed as inevitable — and harmless — as rain to a highlander. Since my books were about outsiders and mystics — men who, by definition, don't give a damn about public opinion or the irrational behaviour of human beings — it would have been illogical to allow all this to depress me. I continued to write *Ritual in the Dark,* and spent my spare time exploring the West country.

In 1957, Cornwall was still something of a backwater. Even in Plymouth, there were still large areas of bomb-damaged houses, and not many new blocks of flats or shops. St. Austell and Mevagissey probably looked exactly as they had in 1900 (when Bernard Shaw used to come down here on holiday). The pubs were shabby, dark and homely, with a tendency to be divided into several small bars and ' dens.' Post-war prosperity was slowly increasing the holiday traffic, but the Cornish had not given much thought to the question of how to exploit it. The quay in Mevagissey was still largely a matter of fish warehouses, with the occasional small shop. It was clear that there was money to be made with commercial acumen, but no one was quite sure how. I even brooded on the idea of opening an ' Angry Young Man ' Coffee Bar and gift shop, and asked John Osborne if he would consider going into partnership with me. Fortunately, he refused. Fortunately, because although I would certainly have made a great deal of money, I would probably have devoted the next ten years to managing the business instead of writing books.

(In fact, it was an old friend of my Soho days, Bill Powell, who started the transformation of Mevagissey into something more like Brighton. One year, he persuaded the harbour board to allow him to set up a stall selling cheap jewellery on the quay ; this was so overwhelmingly successful that he took over a large fish store and turned it into a kind of Marks and Spencers.

This was burnt down a week ago — I am writing this on Christmas Day, 1971 — but it will certainly be rebuilt. Besides, others have now followed in his footsteps ; one of these days, property around Mevagissey harbour will probably be as valuable as in central London).

It took me about six months to get accustomed to the amazing silence of the countryside. Then I began to appreciate it. In New Cross I had lived above a railway line, and after the first night, the trains made no difference at all. Silence was at first more difficult to get used to. And the alone-ness. Sometimes whole days passed without seeing anyone. At nights, there were grasshoppers chirping around the cottage, and an owl in the tree outside the kitchen window. Moths fluttered against the windows and got burnt against the chimneys of the Aladdin lamps. (I had installed an electric generator — in order to run the gramophone — but the batteries were so poor that we tried not to use electric light).

You could follow the brook down the valley over three or four fields, to the sea. Colona Beach was usually covered with pools of cowshit, and masses of drying seaweed. Part of it was ' private,' belonging to the houses on Chapel Point. The story has it that these houses were built by an enterprising architect a few decades ago, but that no one wanted to live in such a remote spot. He committed suicide ; then, one by one, the white Mediterranean-style houses were bought at enormous prices, so they are now our local equivalent of ' millionaires row.'

The beach could be reached by a private road that runs off the bottom of Bodrugan Hill. It runs across Bodrugan land. Mr. Kendall, the farmer at Bodrugan — and one of the biggest local landowners hereabouts — gave us permission to drive down the road. On the first occasion when we did so, an irate gentleman stormed out and asked us who the devil we thought we were.

When we told him we had permission, he became friendly enough. I mention this because a few months ago, I again drove down to Colona Beach, looking for our children ; there were a dozen cars parked there, and the beach was packed with tourists sitting on plastic sheets. I suspect the old gentleman — if he is still alive — has given up the strugggle.

If you turn right at the beach, and walk uphill towards Gorran Haven, you see some of the finest cliff scenery in southern Cornwall. There are long, sheer drops down to the sea, and the usual jagged rocks pointing up at you. One of these rocks, as big as a large house, stands in a hollow in the cliff face ; this is Bodrugan's Leap, from which the farm takes its name. According to the guidebooks, Bodrugan was a supporter of Richard III, and after the battle of Bosworth Field he was ordered by Henry VII to be deprived of his lands. Richard Edgecumbe of Cotehele, his old enemy, came to arrest him at his castle at Bodrugan, and pursued him on horseback towards the cliff edge. Bodrugan spurred his horse over the cliff and onto the great rock below — killing the horse — and then swam out to one of his own boats that conveyed him to France and safety.

Another mile along these cliffs brings you to a point from which you can see Gorran Haven, a small fishing village (where I now live). Like Mevagissey, it is surrounded by hills and cliffs, so that it looks almost too picturesque to be true. I can remember my first walk from Old Walls to Gorran Haven, on the first day we came to look at the cottage. Our nominal ' landlord,' the poet Louis Adeane, was with us. (He rented the cottage from the Kendalls ; financial necessity finally drove him to take a job in London, but he continued to rent the place, dreaming of the day when he would have enough money to return. He never has). On a bright spring morning, I found all this so magical that I could hardly believe my luck. I kept thinking that he was sure to change his mind, now he had seen it again, and decide to return himself . . . And during the two years we lived in Old Walls, I never felt wholly secure, for I could not imagine how anyone could continue to live in London when, with some slight sacrifice of comfort, he could be in this superb place. It was this feeling of insecurity — as well as the need to find a larger place to house my increasing collection of books and records — that led us to look around for a house in 1958. We found one outside Gorran Haven, built only a few years earlier by a retired couple. They had found the loneliness more than they had bargained for, and wanted to get back to the home counties. And so we took the next step in acquiring 'Cornish' nationality by becoming the owners of a house with two acres of land — a step that would have struck me as inconceivable in 1954.

If you walk down to Gorran Haven, and continue along the cliff path, you have to walk waist-deep in ferns for a quarter of a mile, and you find yourself on another beach — Vault, one of the longest in this part of the world. Because it is so inaccessible (i.e. it is impossible to drive a car closer than a quarter of a mile away) this remains fairly deserted ; even in the height of the tourist season, there are seldom more than a few dozen people along its enormous length. And if you care to plod over its yielding pebbles to the far end, you can reckon on total solitude, beyond the reach of the noisiest transistor radio.

I wish to avoid sounding like a guide book, but since this is one of my favourite walks, perhaps I might indulge myself a little further. Assuming you do not want to spend the day on the beach, you can turn right up the hill just before you reach it, and emerge, after a steep climb over a couple of fields, at Lamledra Farm (now a riding stable). It is now possible to continue to follow the shore-line, along a narrow, asphalted road (with a few farm gates to open), above Vault beach. Headlands stick out on both sides. The magnificent, gorse-covered promontary on the right is the Dodman — an ominous-sounding name which actually means a snail. You can walk right out to the point of the Dodman, if you don't mind some rough going, to the great stone memorial cross. which overlooks the sea. I am told — I cannot recall by whom — that this is one of the points around the English coast where Jehovah's Witnesses intend to congregate on the day of Armageddon. I walked out there one dark afternoon a few years ago, and watched a sudden storm blow up. The winds were so high, and the downpour so violent, that we decided to forgo the pleasure of watching the turmoil from the cliff top, and hurried back to the landrover, parked half a mile away. This was a pity. At exactly the time we were on our way back, a boat called the 'Darlwin,' full of holidaymakers, vanished off the

78

Dodman. Against the advice of the harbour-master, she had decided to set out from Fowey to return to Falmouth. She was seen off Mevagissey before the storm, then she simply vanished. What happened, I am fairly sure, is that the bottom of the boat caved in suddenly when they hit a high wave, and she went down like a stone, taking forty passengers, many of them women and children, with her. The boat has never been found ; neither have the bodies, which are probably trapped inside. If we had stayed on the Dodman for ten minutes longer, I might have been able to pinpoint the spot where she disappeared.

Beyond the Dodman, walking enthusiasts can still continue for another mile or so, before they encounter (at Boswinger) the coast road leading to Caerhays and Veryan. In fact, at the bottom of a steep, winding hill, down a road wide enough for only one car, they will discover one of the pleasantest beaches in the area, Hemmick. Because of its enormous rocks — with narrow passageways between some of them — Hemmick has a fairy-tale quality, and children love it. I always go down there after the first storm of the winter, and load up the landrover with drift-wood ; there is usually enough to last me as kindling throughout the winter, and some of the great, heavy spars can be sawed up into logs that burn with a pale blue flame. Hemmick beach is one of our favourite Sunday afternoon excursions. By the time you've walked from one end to the other (preferably at low tide — there are parts where you can easily be caught by a rising tide), and the children have scrambled over rocks and explored small ' caves ' and paddled in the tide pools, everyone is ready for tea, and you have the virtuous feeling that comes from taking exercise.

An equally steep, winding road will take you up to the village of Boswinger, which has a youth hostel and caravan site ; and at this point, the walking scenery is over. You can drive along an attractive (and narrow) coast road, which will take you through Portholland and Portloe — two more tiny fishing· villages — and Veryan and Trewithian, down to St. Mawes, which is Cornwall's bit of French riviera, with expensive hotels, yacht clubs and palm trees. The scenery there is more civilised, with Falmouth just across the water, and St. Michael's Mount and Penzance another half hour's drive down the coast. I am not

particularly fond of these further reaches of south Cornwall —
although I have no dislike of them either. During that first year
we came to Cornwall on holiday — 1954 — I was working in the
office of the Victoria Wine Company in North Finchley, and I
had unearthed a leaflet that advertised mead — the honey drink
of the Anglo Saxons. The manufactory was in Gulval, near
Penzance, and was apparently the site of a monastery. I was so
curious to taste mead that we made Gulval the goal of our
journey. Unfortunately, the firm had gone bust earlier the same
year. The pub next door had mead — in hock-shaped bottles —
on their shelves, but refused to sell us any, saying they wanted to
keep it as a curiosity. So that journey was fruitless. A couple of
years ago, the mead house opened again, this time as a pub, and
we drove down there one Saturday afternoon. It is certainly the
most unusual pub in Cornwall, with great empty stone-flagged
halls leading to the bar, and an atmosphere that is still monastic.
Alas, the only mead they now sell is a sweet, brown stuff like
sherry — pleasant enough, but not the Anglo Saxon nectar
advertised by the old Gulval Mead Company. But I would
recommend anyone to call in there, simply for the sake of
drinking in a pub that looks like a monastery.

I sometimes feel it is absurd that I should be living in
Cornwall. Most of the writers who live in the West country seem
to fit in to the environment — Henry Williamson, Ronald
Duncan, Daphne Du Maurier, Jack Clemo, W. S. Graham — and
it obviously stimulates their writing. But I am not a countryman
by temperament. I am a mystic, but not a nature mystic. My
work is about as ' pastoral ' as Dostoevsky's or Sartre's. When I
lived at Old Walls, I was writing *Ritual in the Dark*, a novel
set in London, and based on the crimes of Jack the Ripper and
of Peter Kürten, the Düsseldorf sadist. I had managed to get hold
of a recording of Berg's Wozzeck from America, and it struck
me then that Berg had tried to do in music what I wanted to do
in prose (at least, in *Ritual*) — to convey a kind of Caligari
world of strain and crisis, of the human mind close to breaking
point. Whenever I walk down that stream from Old Walls to
Colona Beach (as I do sometimes) it reminds me of Wozzeck, and
my own struggles to translate its atmosphere into characters and
events. It seems absurdly inappropriate. Since I have lived in
Cornwall and I have written more than thirty books, a dozen of
them novels. Several of the novels are set in London: two of

them (*The World of Violence* and *The Philosopher's Stone*) in
Leicester. For more than ten years I have been planning and
sketching an enormous novel called *Lulu,* again with Bergian
affinities, which will deal with nature mysticism ; but this will be
set in Sutherland, on the West coast of Scotland.

Yet because Cornwall has been such an enormous part of
my life, because I have lived here and brought up children here,
I suppose it has entered into my bloodstream. The place is
changing fast. When we moved into this house in 1959, there
were fields on four sides of us ; now an enormous housing estate
has been developed between us and the sea (although our house
is high enough to look over it). Every summer, the number of
visitors increases. The huge caravan site at Pentewan has a ' Full
Up' notice on the gate in early July. St. Austell, with its blocks
of new flats, looks like any ' development town ' in the North of
England, and the pubs where we used to be able to drink all
Friday afternoon lost their ' market day ' privileges ten years
ago. There is not a single bar in the area that looks as it
did when I first came here ; all of them have taken to padded
seats and dim red lighting, so they might be in central London.
The Ministry of Transport has promised an extension of the
motorway as far as Truro before the end of the seventies ; when
that happens, we shall have even more visitors, and (presumably)
more crime. (At the moment, there is almost no major crime in
Cornwall — apart from the occasional murder — because the
roads are so bad that getaway would present a real problem).

But I am not saying all this in a tone of complaint. I hardly
ever look out of my windows, so the housing estate doesn't
bother me. I will drink my wine on a padded leather seat just
as happily as on an old fashioned teak bench. I don't spend much
time sunbathing, so the crowds on the beach are a matter of
indifference. The increased number of visitors only bothers me
because some of them call upon me unannounced in the summer
to talk about my books ; but I am arranging to have an electrified
barbed wire fence and guards with machine guns to patrol it.
No, I mention the changes only because it strikes me that fate
was kind in directing me to Cornwall in 1957. For nearly a
decade it remained the peaceful, inefficient, shabby, unexploited
place it had been for centuries, and I saw the last of this. It is

still a highly attractive county, not too crowded, hardly commercialised at all compared to Blackpool or Brighton ; but the twentieth century has definitely arrived. Perhaps in another ten years, I shall feel sufficiently detached to write about the Cornwall I knew when I first came here . . .

8

C. C. Vyvyan

The Lizard

The Lizard peninsula which forms the heel of Cornwall, while Land's End forms the toe and Mount's Bay the sole, measures hardly more than ten miles in any direction. It is, however, full of interest, beauty and associations, and anyone who studies it today will note the rich variety in occupations and diversions of the inhabitants.

There are some large farms and many small holdings; fishing and market gardening which have both declined of late years ; quarrying stone for roads and aerodromes ; quarrying serpentine and making it into small objects as souvenirs for visitors, which are sold in shops in the Lizard village ; jobbing gardeners; hotels and guest houses for summer tourists and " Bed and Breakfast " offered in numberless small houses ; taking tourists out to sea in boats ; dredging for oysters in the Helford river, and also picking winkles ; hunting with the Cury pack of hounds ; roasting an ox once a year at St. Keverne ; lighting Midsummer Night bonfires in high places. Also the district affords a happy hunting ground for those who study wild flowers, geology and archaeology.

Yet if I were asked to describe the country briefly, I should use the single word 'magic.'

It has that same magic which may be felt now and then in the work of great artists, whether it be enshrined in paint or words or marble, that sense of 'something more' behind or beyond or beneath things tangible or visible.

One may feel it in the Hermes of Praxiteles, as he stands alone in a small room of the gallery at Olympia with a marble infant poised on his arm. He has a smile on his face that can hush the exclamations of Americans and cause the heavy-footed Germans to walk softly on their toes, while men of many nations stand still as if they were in church.

One may come across it suddenly, elusive but haunting, in certain lines of poetry.

" the new bathed stars emerge and shine upon the Aral sea."
" The blue Mediterranean where he lay,
Lulled by the coil of his crystalline streams,
Beside a pumice isle in Baie's bay."
" A mermaid on a dolphin's back
Uttering such dulcet and harmonious breath,
That the rude sea grew civil at her song
And certain stars shot madly from their spheres
To hear the sea-maid's music."

Intermittently, in the course of a long life, I have often felt this same magic in certain aspects and qualities of the Lizard peninsula. To imprison those things in words is not an easy task and some of them are dangerously near extinction, threatened by the noise, ugliness and crowds of the industrial age.

Perhaps if we go back in time for more than half a century to a certain summer when I spent many days in that country, I can explain what its atmosphere of magic meant to me then and how it persists now, not only in memory but in actuality. For it was concerned with streams and their secret undergrowth and the coastal track that led along high cliffs and down into valleys, with bird life and wild flowers and moorland space ; and these things have not yet been obliterated in this obliterating age of the bull-dozer.

Nature has changed the cliffs a little since those days, by a land-slide here and there, but only on a small scale. Several of the beaches were polluted with oil from the Torrey Canyon and some have become permanently scarred by the erection of small cafes on their margin. These intrusive little eyesores are useful, no doubt, for quenching the thirst of hundreds of visitors but they have changed the character of the beaches during the summer months. Once they were haunts of permanent peace where the breakers encountered no echoes except their own roar. Now they are trysting places for milling crowds.

On one sandy beach in North Cornwall there is seldom a grain of sand to be seen in fine summer weather ; it becomes populous as any anthill. There is only the over-population of the world to blame. One cannot blame the human ants who are on holiday.

During that summer long ago, my friend B.B., twenty years older than myself and a hundred years wiser, had rented a cottage within the sound of the sea on the Lizard peninsula. The cottage stood in a world's end kind of valley, unfrequented and preserving its own solitude, standing some ten feet above the lane and being guarded by an evergreen hedge. Across the lane was a burbling stream and beyond that a field of sedges and long grass haunted by the ever-croaking notes of the corn-crakes. At night we slept out in the tiny cottage garden and we were out-of-doors all day and every day, and all the time we were free from any tiresome thing, such as an obligation, a purpose or even an objective. We were free and undirected as thistledown. We walked and walked and we noticed every living thing, every fern and flower with an almost possessive delight, any change of shape in a cloud or of colour in the sea. We nearly always kept to the coastal path, for the sea was so beautiful we could not bear to leave it out of sight.

B.B. carried a blackthorn stick and a string bag with our food and I took my bathing dress. Sometimes we lay in the sun on the sand or among the boulders of a beach, and sometimes we made a nest for ourselves on a high cliff, choosing a bed of grass or heather where we could smell the gorse behind us. Sometimes I would bathe, then lie out in the sun to dry in my wet bathing dress and go into the water again to meet the lovely coolness.

Or, at low tide, we would poke about among the sea pools left accessible, looking at the coloured stones and sea anemones and little crabs and shrimps and prawns ; and always we would search for that exquisite seaweed which spreads out rose-pink filaments when under water, making a beautiful filagree pattern. Or we would scramble over wet rocks for the pleasure of hearing the seaweed crackle under our feet, and sometimes we would bring home a trophy of the wide ribbon seaweed, glistening with brine and water, to be hung on the inside of our cottage door and serve as a weather prophet.

From the high cliffs we had often an intimate view of bird life. If we lay very still in our heather nests we could watch the movement all about us of stonechats, whinchats, wheatears and larks ; we might even see a flock of goldfinches. Overhead two ravens might be somersaulting in the air, and far below us, if we looked over the edge, we could watch shags, cormorants, gulls and oyster-catchers. On the beaches we could watch the turnstones at their careful work, and the sanderlings moving swiftly with skating attitudes over the wet sand.

So the days followed each other, each one full of rich experience, and of perfect contentment.

Only once, during an afternoon, did we turn inland and after scrambling up through undergrowth beside a stream, we came out at last to open moorland. We passed over a single road that cuts across the moorland and walked over bog and heather until we were far away, in all directions, from any cultivated or inhabited land. Then we settled down among great clumps of the Cornish heath (erica vagans) and let the silence of Goonhilly Downs take possession of us. It was a wonderful silence, far more full of meaning than any human speech and as we sat without uttering a word, it seemed as if Goonhilly was a brooding presence, a beneficent presence that was setting a seal upon our friendship.

We both felt the same passionate love for wild life and for the freedom that may be found when one is alone under the open sky in uninhabited country. Our close friendship lasted thirty years until her death.

That brooding presence of the Downs was to play an important part in my life, when some years later, I married and came to live near the northern border of that moorland, and found that we owned a considerable part of it. There was, however, never any sense of possessiveness, although my husband gained at one time a good income from his quarries. The allegiance was always on one side and we knew it was a privilege to have such a neighbour.

I owe so much to that wild tract of land. I could now walk into the heart of it in less than an hour, settle down in the heather at a point where there was not a human being or a human dwelling visible and enjoy the blessing of complete solitude ; even in the happiness of married life, that particular moorland solitude had its own magic.

Turning from the subject of magic in the Lizard countryside· to a more factual survey of the peninsula as it is today, one will notice the astonishing changes that have taken place in the last fifty years.

First of all there is the noise. There is no security of silence anywhere. Even the erstwhile solitary and quiet moorland is subject to this curse of the twentieth century, for it is threaded with two main roads that now bear heavy traffic of cars and lorries, while overhead there is constantly the drone or roar or penetrating shriek of aeroplanes from Culdrose. This aerodrome created in World War Two, is manned by the Royal Navy and was very unpopular at first because it occupied some of the best agricultural land in the district. Today however everyone pays tribute to the wonderful sea-rescues performed by Culdrose helicopters. We also recognise the fact that its existence has increased the population and prosperity of the district. It straddles the neck of the peninsula from Gweek at the head of the Helford river to Gunwalloe on the coast. One can walk from estuary to open sea in about an hour.

A few miles beyond this neck and just beyond the northern boundary of Culdrose is the town of Helston, formerly a busy railway terminus that handled a large trade in rabbits and market garden produce and tourists. Today the railway is closed for passenger traffic ; the luckless inhabitants and visitors of the Lizard's extremities have to go over twenty miles to catch a train at Redruth, Penzance or Falmouth and the connections between railway and local 'buses are hopeless. Helston is the metropolis for the Lizard country which possesses about twenty villages but no town.

The nearest village to Gweek is Mawgan-in-Meneage, so-called by this clumsy name to distinguish it from the Mawgan near Newquay. The word 'Meneage' means 'stony' and the word 'Lizard' means a high or a steep place.

Another great change, perhaps as important as the development of noise, is the defacement of the land. That small territory, surrounded by salt water on three sides, has now to bear a heavy burden of human erections, none of which is beautiful. There are relics of two world wars, set up for defence or observation and now become unsightly survivals; concrete bases, disused pylons and nissen huts converted into many strange purposes, all scattered about in odd places. And there are Council Houses. No new town has sprung up in that area to serve the needs of the increased population, but Helston has spread out in every direction in order to cope with this problem; and now each village, as if it were some egg-laying creature, is spawning new houses at a speed that seems to be inevitable and cancerous.

The need is urgent and speed is not often allied with creation of beauty or with good workmanship. These huddles and straight lines of houses are often replicas of each other and the last one built seems to be more exactly like the rest of them than any other, if that were possible. They seem to be looking with malevolent aspect on the old thatched and whitewashed cottages that are falling into decay one by one.

There are also new bungalows scattered about the land like warts or carbuncles.

Finally, there has now appeared in the heart of Goonhilly Downs, that solitary place hitherto frequented only by a few snipe-shooters, fox-hunters, bird-watchers and devotees of silence a modern miracle, up-ended. It is in the form of three enormous, silver-coloured saucers standing on their edges and each provided with a swivel. This new inhabitant of the lonely moorland has come to stay; it has the power of hearing instantaneous messages from all round the world.

Goonhilly Downs is the home of Telstar.

There are also changes that cannot be measured or enumerated. The feudal spirit is dying out, but what is far more important is that we are losing some of the kindliness of heart that we once possessed, becoming less generous and less hospitable, more suspicious of strangers; and, when we do face the fact that many of us are becoming curmudgeons, we blame it on the tourist trade.

Even more significant than those things is the decline in the use of dialect. The causes of this are not far to seek. Easier communications with the increase of cars, the influx of evacuees into private homes during the last war, the mass invasion of our summer tourists and, finally, the opening of the Tamar bridge: all these things have contributed to rendering the Cornish less Cornish. In the Lizard peninsula, as elsewhere, you may see the young people look askance with shame when their parents use Cornish words.

One of the strongholds of dialect was the single-plank bench fixed against a wall in Cadgwith and in continual use in the good years of the fishing business. It was always sacred to the elder fishermen, for it overlooked the little beach of the little cove, also the arrival and departure of boats, the ebbing and the flowing of the tides and a V-shaped vista of the open sea. The old men used to settle there like snails in a wall, or elders in council, while they exchanged news and memories and forecasts of the weather and criticism of the Government.

It was the local parson who introduced me to those veterans on a day when he had taken me out mackerel fishing in his boat. He was a man as notable for his prowess among the life-boat crew as for his commendable brevity in the pulpit. His 'star turn' sermon lasted exactly three minutes.

After that introduction, I always felt that I had friends in Cadgwith, and to listen to those old sea-dogs talking in broad Cornish was like listening to music. Their stories and their comments were more often old than new, for they were very fond of repeating themselves. There was the endearing rogue 'Boy Joe' who, according to his friends, "would pinch the buttons off your trousers." He would invariably encounter this accusation with a ready quip that was full of pride mingled with only half-assumed indignation: "Well, ef I ded take theare net off Jimmy Choak every waun der knaw as how he helps hisself reg'lar-like from the Doctor's crabbin' pots."

Then there was Sam Trencer who was shaped like a barrel and had an equal capacity for holding his beer. He did not speak much, but whenever a conger was mentioned he would relate his own special story. "I tuk in a conger waunce, hauled un in an'laid un in the bilge, an' 'e rawse up an' stood theare in the middle of the boat an' 'e barked like a dog; 'e was the biggest conger any man ever seed. Oogly oal fish they be." Also there were the twin brothers, John-Charles and Ignatius Lobb. Nobody could tell them apart until Ignatius was left with a single front tooth while John-Charles had two teeth and a half. John-Charles was never known to speak more than two words at a time but Ignatius had a fund of stories and a rich vocabulary.

On politics he had little to say, for his creed was simple. "I aan't no Conservative an' I never will be. All the gentry is Conservative an' I dare say what's good for the gentry caan't be good for we." He would often add: "Darn them Conservatives, they aan't no good an' the Socialists aan't no good neether. I've got to pay for my loaf o' bread whichever side wins, so it's no good votin' anyways."

On the subject of fish and fishing and the ways of women he was always oracular. "There be all kinds of fishermen," he told us. "There be some what takes a lighted candle outside the kitchen door an' ef et der blaw out they wean't go to sea. Over to Coverack now, there be two kinds o' fishermen, them what wears out their jerseys in front, leanin' 'pon the wall, an' them what wears out the seat of their trousis settin' down at home. But I've been to sea at nights weth Cadgwith men what could lean over the gunnel and tell where we was to, weth nawthen but the breakers to guide them."

On the subject of women there was endless talk but there was always one point of agreement. "When there's fish caught the women wean't say nawthen, not ef you was to go overstairs in your seaboots, for they der knaw shure nuff that when fish scales der come to bed there's money in the 'ouse."

On one other topic there was general agreement and that concerned a certain type of tourist who tried to patronize the Cornish people. A perfect specimen of these creatures approached the Stick (as the Bench was called) one day, strolling down from her guest-house on the hill as if the place belonged to her. She was waving a silly-looking ornamental cane that was hardly strong enough to strike down a nettle and her clothes were like those of the very young, except for a floppy Dolly Varden hat, while her face was middle-aged. Ignatius was in the middle of a good story about a shoal of pollock but he stopped dead as she came near. He fixed his eyes on the sea. She stopped in front of the seated men. " Good day," she said, and she put on an intimate smile addressed to each one of them. " Good day," one or two of them replied and then looked to a ship on the horizon.

" Taking a nice rest I see," she said brightly.

There was a dead silence. It seemed as if the eloquence of Ignatius and the animated attention of the others had been turned off suddenly by a switch.

" You poor dear men," she said, " you must have a dreadful life always at sea on dark winter nights while we sleep, snug in our little beds."

The men sat still as images.

" You poor darlings," she went on, " working so hard to get our food." Then, rather nervously, trying to break the silence, she went on: " He! He! He! I daresay if you'd only talk you'd have some dreadful tales to tell of your dangers and adventures."

" Miss," said Ignatius, and he took his black pipe from his mouth and spat respectfully into the road before he said what he had to say: " Have 'ee ever looked out o' your front door an' seen comin' in the bay a boat with waun man instead o' two? I seed un waunce an' I never shall forget it. 'Tes a oogly thing fur to see. The wimmen, they was tremblin' all over on the beach, all except the waun woman who saw her one man in the boat.

91

an' when he come in shore he said: ' Iss friends, Joe's gone weth the pots' ".

I did not hear the stranger's comments, for at that moment the parson appeared with a string of mackerel in each hand and I had to go with him to help in the distribution.

I cannot remember any other group of people other than those veterans of the "Stick" who habitually and unself-consciously kept dialect alive.

There were, however, as there still are, individuals who spoke habitually in the Cornish sing-song and enriched their talk with strange Cornish words. There was the barber, a man of parts and a gifted mimic, who was a popular figure renowned for telling stories in dialect at local entertainments. Once he used this gift with telling effect on a female client when he was shampooing her. She was a stranger, another of the gushing type whose holiday enthusiasm expressed itself in ill-chosen and unwelcome words about ' the quaintness of these dear Cornish people.' We may be peculiar but we do not need a foreigner to tell us that we are.

"Such lovely voices they have, these dear Cornish people," she said to him. " I do love to listen to their talk. It's so quaint — like something in a book."

He made no reply but went on rubbing her head with the towel, bringing his fingers ever lower until they nearly encircled her neck and then pressing his thumbs in violently until she shrieked.

" Aw me deearr," he said, assuming a loud, raucous tone. " I beg your pardon. Ded I gov'ee a scat on the huddick? A proper antic, baan't it?"

" What did you say?" she murmured in a frightened voice from the folds of the towel, but he only went on rubbing furiously and when she stood up to pay the bill, he shouted in the same loud voice: " Tol'ble dry in the oozle deear."

She fled from the shop. When she got back to her guest-house she confided the experience to her landlady who happened to be the barber's cousin. Thereafter he often included this story

92

against himself in his talks on Cornwall and the audience always thought it did him credit.

There is also a farmer's wife, still living, whose Cornish accent is perfect. She is a highlight at a certain annual tea when she relates, with suitable variations, her story of " Killing a Pig " — an operation known locally as ' puttin' away a pig,' ' putting ' being pronounced like putting in golf.

A single glance at the map will show that the Lizard country is dominated by three features: the rocky coast line which contains all the south and west of the land, Helford river and Goonhilly Downs.

As for the rocky coast, one cannot realise its magnificence until one views it from the sea. There was a day when a local friend, an old sea-dog, took us out from Cadgwith in his motor-boat to land on Mullion island. As we rounded the Lizard point the tide came pouring out of Mount's Bay as from a funnel and we were wallowing in rough water where wind and tide met one another. Then in a few minutes we were in smooth water again. We steamed ahead, passing Lion Rock and Rill Ledges and Vellan Head and Predannack. The cliffs were seamed with caves and fissures and jutting rocks and every landmark had its own history. Ravens were croaking and somersaulting in the air overhead. We followed the curves of the bay while the skipper told us local stories.

" That narrow slit," he said, " is the sheep-stealer's cave ; plenty of thieving in those days. They always said if you put a hot loaf on the horns of a cow you could twist the horns any way and then the owner wouldn't know his own beast . . . Sir Richard climbed that rock, the one like a top-hat. He couldn't get down and he had to dive into the sea . . . there's the cove that got Billy Trevena his beating. He'd a mind to go to the Fair but they took him fishing and he said to his father when they got to the mouth of the cove, " Look, there's a fox." 'Siah put back of course. No fisherman will go to sea if he sees a fox. The lad went to the Fair but he got his beating too . . . that crack is called Marmaduke — no, I can't tell you why."

Many a smuggling yarn he told us also, but when we mentioned wrecking, his mouth shut like a trap. Wrecking is a delicate subject for any Cornishman.

Meanwhile we were watching the rocky face of the coast. It was new and strange seeing familiar spots from the sea. We saw the sea birds in their haunts, guillemots and razorbills huddled in their crevices or flying, swift as any shuttle, out to sea ; shags and cormorants with snaky silhouettes or spread-eagled wings ; hundreds of herring gulls flying about ; great black-backed gulls with beak and eyes that have no pity.

We were looking at a section of the bowels of the earth, the tortured twisted, broken strata of rock, memento of primeval cataclysms. We could see where hornblende and schist gave way to serpentine. The earth was giving up its secrets.

We came to a tiny bay in Mullion island. The sea was heaving gently beneath long ribbons of brown seaweed rooted in the rock. We scrambled ashore and I climbed to the highest point of the little island. On the mainland, less than a mile away, were the Marconi poles, slender giants set up for seizing and concentrating power, now etched upon the sky. The rocks were white and slimy with bird droppings. I perched on the highest crag and might have been alone on Everest ; but I was not alone, for there came a babel of sound from quite a hundred gulls that rose from below and circled about like lost spirits. The whirl of wings gave me a strange exultant feeling, as if, for a moment, I was lord of sea and space. The things of earth had receded into some abyss unseen. For one instant I was on the brink of infinity, no tangible object being of any importance.

When I returned to the boat the skipper was knocking out his pipe before he pulled up the anchor. On the way home he stopped the engine and we backed slowly into Dollar Ugo cave. The water at the entrance was deep purple, begotten of black overhanging rock and green water. Coming out from that mysterious place into the world of life and light, we steamed on until we came to another cave, open to the sky, the Devil's Frying-Pan. Martins were flying to and fro from their cup-like nests of mud that were attached to the vaulted entrance. Over-head we could see flowers of the brilliant sea-aster, beautifying crevices.

Now the dramatic smuggling days are ended, wrecks are broken up by the rocks, and legends are fading out ; but the martins, as usual, will be speeding south at Michaelmas, and year after year the aster in some crevice will multiply and bloom, looking down upon the surging sea.

The Helford river needs a volume to itself. Some people who know the river well regard its shores as holy ground. One should row up river, quite alone, on a rising tide, from the mouth to Gweek, as I did the first time I explored it. I was rowing along slowly on a waterway paved with green reflections of the quiet fields and sapling oaks. There was no other boat to break the silence. Nor was there any other movement except the spasmodic movements of the river's natural inhabitants. The river was their world and it belonged to them. There were shelducks and dabchicks, swans now and then flying overhead with the exquisite music of their beating wings ; herons croaking from a tree or standing sentinel in shallow water, and once the brilliant flash of a kingfisher. The river narrowed gradually but the silence grew ever deeper and I began to feel that I was rowing into infinity.

Since then, attempts have been made to break that silence. A plan was formed to dam the upper part of the river and make a yachting pool for tourists. Another scheme was to convert an ancient boat-house into a buffet that would serve ' de luxe ' suppers and thereby lure visitors to come up the river in speed boats. Both plans fell through, the first from the force of public opinion, the second from a change of heart in the planners.

How long will it be before another vandal comes forward to shatter the peace of the river ? At present it is unspoiled from Abraham's Bosom to Gweek. From that Bosom to the open sea there is another tale to tell, but at any rate there are four beautiful gardens, over fifty years old, each one in a little valley running down to the water.

The lonely moorland is less spectacular than the coast and less dramatically enchanting than the river. It is aloof and austere. It bears no traffic of boats or cars. You make your own path through the heather, with never a beaten track to help you. You can still settle down in the heart of the moorland where

95

there is no human dwelling in sight. There you can put off the straight-jacket of your own identity, achieving blissful unity with the earth. If you crush a sprig of bog myrtle, its scent will bring you near to the spirit of wildlife. No gardenia bloom, nor tuberose, nor frangipani is so evocative.

There are people who find Goonhilly Downs a gloomy, monotonous place. Others deplore that it does not lend itself to development, to use that sinister umbrella-word nowadays employed by profiteering man when he plans some improvement on nature or some destruction of beauty. Fortunately the qualities of the place, its spaciousness and beauty and powers of inspiration are not for sale.

Speaking personally of Goonhilly, it has always been a beloved presence in my life, ever since that day when B.B. and I listened in to the deep silence there. Its presence is like that of a close friend who is always " there " even in absence. The magic of the country has not failed or faded.

How, a number of people may be asking, can the Lizard with all those mundane occupations and diversions of the people, retain its magic? I can only affirm that the magic is still there for those who are responsive. Possibly it will remain there, in spite of Telstar, Culdrose and the recent plantations of uncongenial conifers, so long as mankind does not deface the natural features.

Yet, if you want to renew your sense of that magic, you will do well to wander alone, and preferably in winter, whenever you visit the Helford river, the rocky coast and the lonely moorland.

9

Arthur Caddick

Nancledra

Nancledra is the first village on the Cucurrian, the red river, after it rises from Amalveor Downs on the slopes of Trendrine hard by Buttermilk Hill. The source of the Cucurrian, springing from granite and crystalline rock, is hidden by furze and heath and bracken, and its watershed is a hill which is part of the majestic barricade which seals off the prehistoric interior of the last length of the Land's End peninsula before the Cornish earth dives abruptly into the Atlantic.

Nancledra is almost equidistant from Zennor, St. Ives and Penzance. In the centre of the village, just over the bridge, there still stands an ancient building which, centuries ago, was the cause of the grouping round it of cottages and barns and stables. This is Nancledra Mill, now protected as an historic building. Inside it, you may still see the formidable construction, driven by the power of water, the like of which crushed corn for well-nigh all the generations of man until the coming of the machine ; outside, you may see the rusty grills of the old sluice-gate, and the shrunken and shallow vestige of the mill-pool.

The Cucurrian river winds down from Nancledra past Boskennal Mill, then through Ludgvan woods, in a deep granite chasm cut by the breaking of glaciers at the end of the Ice Age, and reaches the sea near Marazion.

Between the two mills, there stands, rather decrepitly, a gigantic tin-wheel which once whirled its attached buckets round and round through the river, so that the streamers could wash away the dirt from their tin. Misleadingly, the old Cornish name for a wheel such as this is a Stamp, and the village people still so call it. These wheels, however, have no connection at all with tin-stamping. From time immemorial, this stamping was regulated by the Crown, under the Stannary Laws, and strict control was enforced through the Charter granted to the coinage-towns. Tin ingots, in the old days, were as jealously guarded as is gold bullion now. All the same, the Nancledra tin-wheel is a Stamp to Nancledra people, and it will probably remain so till the Doom.

Above Nancledra, towards St. Ives, there is another much more prominent legacy from the mining past, the engine-house, with its tall chimney, of Giew Mine. For a short time, after the 1918 Armistice, this was the only tin-mine then working in Cornwall, and its great heyday is part of local legend. In those days of boom, there were two inns in Nancledra village itself ; there are none now. Giew Mine dominates the skyline at Cripple's Ease, near Cuckoo Hill, the one so named because of the stone through a hole in which children with rickets used to be pushed in the past, so that the magic of the movement might bring a cure, the other, because it is the fabled site of the bush where men of Towednack Parish danced round and round and round, to keep a cuckoo in so that summer might linger with them forever. Towednack Church, the Parish Church of Nancledra, is said to have taken an unconscionable time a-building, because the Devil took up the restrictive practice of mounting the scaffolding each night to hurl down the granite masonry put into place each day. However, though the Parish failed in its plan to capture an eternal summer, it did manage, at last, to beat the Devil, and the solid tower of the Church stands foursquare to all the winds to prove it.

You will by now have noticed that this is no place for sufferers from frayed nerves, and I have one more horror still to relate. One of the most baleful and maleficent stones of all Cornwall's tale of recorded time once stood stark in the heart of Nancledra. It was a large, high, circular boulder with a flat top. On this evil circle once foregathered all the Witches in Cornwall, on Midsummer's Eve, to exchange vile counsels, hatch black mischief, brew baleful herbal spells, and work mincing mallicho, and dance round and round in sinful postures, like demented dervishes of the caste of " Hair." Happily for the virtue of One & All, this Albert Hall of Black Magic was dynamited into derisive dust when the ground was cleared for the Village Hall.

At this point I think it prudent to placate the protagonists of rationality ; some of the legends preserved in Nancledra folk-memory have a less metaphysical basis than the mephitic infamies I have just stooped to repeating. On the eastern slope of the sharp descent into Nancledra from Penzance, there is a field called, by immemorial tradition, Battle. It falls sharply down to the Cucurrian. A quarter of a century ago, I was out walking and I met a very old Cornish farmer. We fell to talking, and, presently, he told me that this field once ran red with blood downalong into the red river. I believed him, then, because it was pleasant to do so. I believe him, now because, over the years, innumerable flint arrow-heads have been ploughed up in this Field of Battle. But I have not yet come to take as truth another ancient Cornish legend — that St. Joseph of Arimathaea once walked this way.

Nancledra is surrounded by evidences of antiquity so remote that the imagination falters in seeking to visualise it. If, for instance, you happen to wander round Oxford, the Renaissance warms felicitously into life behind the mullions, and beneath the towers and spires, and the arched gates of the Lodges at the Colleges. And if, perchance, you stroll through the walled City of York, where Caesar, himself, sat in judgement, and Ulpian, the great jurisconsult, sat in Court in the course of a circuit which started at Byzantium, you may feel — I certainly did — the imponderable weight of the grandeur that was Rome bearing inexorably down upon you. In West Penwith, however, if you climb the earth ramparts thrown up by Celtic tribesmen to fortify Tren Crom, or climb the hill where Castle-an-Dinas still defies the outrage of one of the worst scars ever inflicted upon Cornwall by the quarrying of stone, you cannot — I surely cannot — as the modern jargon goes " identify." This past is so old, so still, so cold ; as old as Stonehenge, as silent as the gravestones of Lanyon Quoit, as cold as the bottom of the Levant Mine.

99

To raise your spirits after all this mortality, I now turn myself from an historian to a human being once more, and proclaim that Nancledra, to-day, is as lively as you make 'em. It nourishes a boisterous Youth Club, a first-class Young Farmers' Club, and, of course, and thank Heaven fasting, a W.I. This is the dynamo that generates good works and fosters the learning of skills, and it is the energy of the women in the village that drives it forever. How immeasurably poorer and more humdrum would village life in this kingdom be if there were no Women's Institutes!

Although we arrived in Cornwall in 1945, I share with all my family the belief that our Cornish life did not start properly until we had moved into Windswept Cottage, Nancledra, in 1946. For the two youngest of my children this is the literal truth ; we lugged all our belongings to Windswept, from a furnished cottage higher up, taking the old track across the croft as our route, in August, 1946. My third daughter was born on a radiant afternoon in August, 1947 ; my second son blew in upon us, in my study, on a gusty morning, Trafalgar Day, in 1948. This prompted our cheerful village grocer to nickname him Nelson.

I daresay nobody but the utterly feckless and the abysmally shiftless would have behaved as we did ; we moved into a cramped four-roomed cottage, with three young children, and then proceeded practically to double the density of infant population at the hair-raising rate of one a year, on the dot. Well that is what we did, and we have had no regrets at all, save that I sometimes attribute my longevity to not being dead, and at other times feeling a mordant pang, and wince, as I recall a day when I started to correct a pile of nappies, mistaking them for galley-proofs. All the same, we did sometimes stare blankly at each other, my wife and myself, by the fire late at night, and wonder why the cottage seemed to shrink every day, and doubled its speed of diminution in the winter. Space is magnified by the light of summer suns, but winter darkness makes it dwindle. This is a discovery older than Einstein, and may be expressed as the Law of the Seasonal Relativity of Relatives ; they seem more so in the shortest days. On a wet day, it sometimes crossed my mind that I had more sons clomping about the home than the sons in one of those Old Testament genealogies

which start with Adam and never end ; you know the ones —
somebody begets somebody after every comma. In spite of
everything, we managed not to suffocate each other, thanks, I
am sure, to my master-plan of running our family as a
democracy — tempered by a dictatorship. I profoundly dis-
believe in letting children tell their parents what to do — well,
not this parent, anyhow. For a large family, life in a small space
is impossible unless there is a system of manners — and Pa has
the Veto, and the Casting Vote, and the right to banish rebellious
citizens of the home temporarily to the exile of bed.

I acquired Windswept as a family home by moving into it
as a Service Tenant of the old Cornwall Electric Power
Company. With the cottage went the keys and custody of a
vertical slab of cement. This was the Sub-Station, and it serviced,
among other places, the pumps at Geevor Mine, and the Land's
End Radio Station. Consequently, it always had to be attended
by somebody right on the spot, who became myself. " Bottom,
thou art translated!" I was summoned to emergency duty, at
any time of the day or night, by a titanic alarm-bell in our
bedroom. "Art thou poor, and hast thou golden slumbers?"
The bell rattled like a machine gun and everything in the
bedroom rattled with it as its thunderous tocsin shook the
cottage, much as the hunchback's tolling shook the belfry of
Notre Dame. I would dive at the bell out of dreams and switch
it off. Then I had to hare like hell over the croft to the Sub-
Station, and peer at a spectral array of dials, until the hand of
one of them revealed to me what had blown up and where.
I then telephoned Control at Hayle Power Station, and told
them the worst. Thereafter, I usually had to take out enormous
switches (I racked them out with a lever over a run of cogs)
to isolate faulty sections of the line. Then I had to ascertain
that a meticulous code of safety-precautions had been followed
to the last iota, before the gang of linesmen started their tour
of inspection of the section to find the fault. They would swarm
up towering poles in darkness, often with a seventy-mile-an-hour
gale lashing rain into their faces, and might have to patrol and
climb throughout the night, and then all the next day, to restore
supply to Cornish homesteads and factories and farms and hotels,
all the vast diversity of means by which the Cornish earn their
living. (An anxious mother in the village once called breathlessly

upon me, in a raging sou'-wester of a gale, to ask me to put the lights on for her boy's homework, because of the Eleven-Plus). All the linesmen I knew were Cornish, the toughest and most loyal men I have ever worked with ; they became my friends, and I was proud of it, and they took to asking my wife to heat for them some of the toughest and most lethal Cornish Pasties I have ever seen.

I suppose the Sub-Station might be described as a glorified fuse-box. Something blew when an overhead or earth fault developed, and a dial would register which it was, and on what stretch of line. I solemnly contracted with the Cornwall Electric Power Company to hold myself available at all times of the day and night, including Bank Holidays, and Sundays, and I undertook never to desert my action-station without getting prior permission, by phone, from the Control Officer at Hayle. And I kept my bargain. For the whole of my first year with the Company, I contented myself with going out for a drink every eighth Saturday only. This saved money, and restored my ravaged liver ; I tilled my $\frac{7}{8}$ acre of land like mad and learnt to use my hands for the first time in my life. Happily my sanity was saved by a wide relaxation of my hermit-like regime at the suggestion of the Company, at the end of the first year.

On leaving, I was given a Certificate of "seven years satisfactory Service at all times." But this did not please me one millionth as much as the Company's description of my seven-year status as "An Isolator of Bus-Bars." Good God, and I never knew it! I still don't know what Bus-Bars are, though I wish it meant licensed Buses to Penzance. I did just as I was told, and never tried to be clever, and learned to be useful. Meanwhile, I assume the Bus-Bars isolated themselves ; certainly, I never consciously sent the poor things to Coventry.

It was a strange job ; there might be four or five weeks with nothing whatever to recall Electricity to my recollection. Then, in the small hours, pandemonium would be unleashed in our bedroom, and I might find myself doing a hectic and continuous twelve-hour stint of switching and phoning, when a major breakdown cropped up. Very often, the trouble was lightning. The nightmare that bedevilled our thoughts was the fact that all the telephone lines to the Sub were very exposed. Very often, the same thunder-storm that broke a supply-line blew the phone at the same time. Then it was my horrible duty to trot down the steep hill to the village phone, to seek instructions from Control; some times, the village phone had also been blown out. It was then a question of waiting, incommunicado, until a Post Office Engineer arrived. I remember a night when I had to try to close a switch on a fault; the Post Office man suddenly said that he would prefer to go outside, and watch this insane proceeding from a safe distance. I gave the laugh of a superior person, and watched this craven conduct his retreat. Then I banged the switch in. It blew up, and a hail of fragments of porcelain insulators hit me, and everything around me. Luckily they missed my eyes; but the damage took the maintenance-men forty-eight hours to repair. I had one accident only, as an Isolator of Tram Cars. I injured my right hand on a defective switch. It soon got better. (Then, seven years later, paralysis started, and I was operated on). For two months I had my arm in plaster, (which everybody at the Sloop and the Castle and the Kiddleywink, in St. Ives, were gracious enough to autograph for me). Then on Christmas Eve, I got an out-of-the-blue cheque for £99.10.0, in settlement of my claim for personal injury. Yuletide became for my family, transported, regardless, to town in a taxi, a floating paradise of toys, and rum, and clothes, and rum, and rum and lots of candies, and a mountainous heap of fripperies and gew-gaws which gripped us in their useless thrall.

I remember another night, when I had to rush down to the village phone with all the hills around us flashing white in a sizzling, hissing, circle of lightning. When I reached the village it was not, as usual, abed at that hour. Lights were on all over and men were waiting at the police-station gate. The grim tidings had just come to them that a fine village lad had been drowned on the treacherous North coast off Hayle. When I see summer lightning even now, the memory of that desolate drowning still disturbs me.

Such, then, was the ideal job for a struggling writer, that I filled for seven years, with a rent-free cottage, a modest weekly solatium, and almost an acre of rich land, which filled the stomachs of my children with fresh and varied vegetables. These benefits counter-balanced for me the neolithic earth closet in a shed in the garden. It was in this inconvenience that I saw my first Cornish adder. The very month we moved in, I was seated alone in glory, when twenty inches of viper insinuated themselves under the door. I jumped on to the seat like a grasshopper, threw my trousers to their fate, and grabbed a spade I kept in the closet. I cut off the head of that snake with a drive to middle-and-leg, and since that serpent breathed its last I have never stooped to any sort of aperient ; the memory works just as well. In Cornwall, you know, no matter what time you kill them, adders do not die till sundown. My victim must have lived several hours without a head.

Before it was leased to the Electric Power Company, Windswept was a cottage tied to a nearby farm, Borea. The buildings are said to be of the same period, late Tudor. I have not yet sought documents to verify this ; certainly, Windswept is very much older than most of the cottages in the immediate neighbourhood. There is a well, long ago sealed-up, under the stairs, and when we moved in there was, next to the Cornish range, a very old bread-oven, in which slices of turf were once burnt for the baking. The combined flue for the range and the oven was six feet wide at the base, and went back over three feet to the outerwall.

I often chide myself, now, for not having had the bread-oven photographed and carefully measured before I took it out. We needed the space it filled ; four men could have sat on chairs round a table in the base of the chimney, and played poker without undue discomfort. I managed to remove all the granite walls myself, except the end wall of the oven jutting out into the room. A neighbour of ours, a quarryman, came to our rescue and tackled this. It was a single granite slab six feet high, and he estimated its weight as over half a ton. It supported a massive square of granite on its summit, which protected the bedroom-floorboards from fire. Our neighbour had to reduce the wall-stone to boulders of a hundredweight and a half or so before he could roll them out of the front door. I recall one of my daughters at the sound of the hammer and the chisel and the axe, scuttling under her bed for her cover. Cornishmen seem to think that slicing-up granite slabs is a totally-silent, parlour-game sort of task. Some of the boulders were built into a wall near my window, and look very handsome indeed when the sun catches their facets after rain.

Hammered between two stones as a wedge, I found, when I was taking the oven away, a horseshoe with an elongated, rather delicate shape. It seems that horses were shod with shoes of this shape only up to the eighteenth-century, when the breed came in that is shod, to-day, with squatter and more circular shoes. I put this horseshoe away somewhere so safe that I have lost it forever.

I found, also, and this had also been used as a wedge, a heavy cast-iron octagon, about three-and-a-half inches at its greatest width. Another neighbour, Jimmy Martin, told me that it was a " kook," that is to say, a quoit, and that his grandfather had often told him that "kook" was a game he had never seen played since his boyhood. When he told me this, Jimmy was nearly seventy, so his grandfather's boyhood might easily date back to a time somewhere near to the year of the Battle of Waterloo.

I got to know Jimmy Martin well, and this took a considerable time, even after he had been doing our running repairs for months, and had grown used to our habit of producing cups of tea whenever we felt like it — five minutes after he'd made a morning start, or in the middle of mixing cement, or when he needed one of the boys to hold a ladder. He was taciturn and withdrawn by nature, and I am sure that this was rooted in shyness. No doubt deafness emphasised his mood. But he gradually came to feel at home with us, and, sometimes when he was drawing on a pipe that should have been impounded for pollution, he would regale us with droll tales of his youth. One made a vivid impression on me. It seems that Towednack Vicarage was due for extensive repairs and decorations, and the contractor who had landed the fat job was not precisely scrupulous about his quantities in such things as plaster-mixing, and cement, and mortar. The Ecclesiastical Commissioners had engaged a London architect to supervise the work, and on his first visit he arrived in a top-hat just after a very considerable mixing of concrete. He marched up to the mixture, took a pinch of it between his fingers, and let it run through them to the ground. " Sub-standard-breach of contract — condemned —

remix," he announced and drove off without another word in a pony and trap. This happened several times, with several materials, and the contractor felt cheated of his customary sidelines of profit. So when the dining-room was to be replastered, with first-class material, he ordered his men — it was the height of summer — to report for work the next day two hours early, at six o'clock, so that he could steal a march. The architect usually appeared at ten o'clock. So the workmen got two long and high walls plastered, and the contractor was feeling a new man. Then, at eight o'clock the architect marched in. He gazed at the fresh and gleaming plaster. Then he took his silver-topped cane and walked round the room and slashed the plaster diagonally and made a total wreck of it. He wiped his cane on a newspaper, and said: "Sub-standard — breach of contract — condemned — remix — contractor to bear expense," and walked off. For the first time in his career, the contractor was meted out scrupulous justice and never got over the shock.

My first encounter with Jimmy had been disconcerting, more, exasperating. I had been told he was available for odd jobs, because he had retired from his duties as head carpenter, chief mason, and foreman — bricklayer, at a farm nearby worked by an ex-Wing Commander. Actually, Jimmy was the total staff of one, but the Winco must have been satisfied for he invited him to stay on as long as he liked. Jimmy was skilled in many trades — he was a past-master in the ancient Cornish craft of hedge-building from stone — and he did not know such a thing as demarcation had been invented. What is more, he hated working slowly.

So I called at his bungalow at the bottom of our lane, which he had built single-handed in the Twenties, and asked him if he'd be good enough to look at our Cornish range, the most infuriating piece of apparatus I had ever encountered in all my life. Nothing much was wrong with it — except that either no fire could be lit at all, or, if it could, no fire would stop smoking till we doused it.

"I'll be up-along d'rectly, Capun," said Jimmy.

A week went by; I called to remind him.

"Be up-along d'rectly, Capun," he replied again.

A few days later, still with a wistful ghost of hope on her

face, my wife remarked: "I asked in the village. D'rectly is Cornish for 'very soon'."

' It must be archaic usage, then," was my answer.

We ploughed through another morass of Hades with our range. Again, I called on Jimmy.

This time, Mrs. Martin was alone in the bungalow.

" My man do say to tell you he'll be up-along d'rectly," she told me.

I thanked her and left, and trudged " home to the range, where seldom is heard a discouraging word, and the skies are not cloudy all day." Unlike Bing Crosby, I had no song at all left in my bleeding heart.

I asked Jimmy once more, but he never came.

Not long after we'd finally given him up, I found out, accidentally why. To guard against a tell-tale in the village, he had stopped doing any work at all in this district. He'd become a Regional Old-Age Pensioner, that is to say, he had decided that work he did outside his home district, did not count, and need not be declared against his Pension, for the perfectly-good Cornish reason that the odds against being found out were big enough to gamble on.

This was not dishonesty at all ; far from it. Jimmy was scrupulously honest in personal dealings man-to-man. But man-to-man does not include Them, Authority in any shape or form. In Cornwall, every Tax-Law is passed by Parliament so that the Cornish may have the pleasure of breaking it. It is a legacy of their Free-Trading days, when the Brandy-Men drove the Riding-Men over the boundaries of Cornwall and past the borders of sanity. During the Napoleonic Wars, Pitt had to cope with not only the Corsican Ogre, but also the Cornish contraband. The latter never met its Waterloo.

A more profound reason why Jimmy kept putting me off was that he was a Celt through and through. He disliked disappointing people. By now, I have come to grips with this habit so I can usually allow for it. It is irritating, but I become more and more convinced that it is not cussedness but a sign of an innate gentleness of heart. Celtic people take no pleasure in dealing-out pain of any sort, even the most trivial.

Like many thousands of Cornishmen of his generation, before the First World War, Jimmy Martin had gone to America to find work. Poverty drove the most ambitious of the Cornish abroad, anywhere where mountains waited to be moved and ores of any sort to be mined. Jimmy had almost lost his hearing digging the foundations for Chicago skyscrapers. In those days there were no sophisticated means of equalising underground and surface pressures. Countless young Cornishmen jumped at the offer of thirty shillings an hour " danger-money," and descended with simple faith, to work with pick and shovel and axe and dynamite deep in the bowels of the earth. Jimmy told me how a young friend of his had suddenly screamed out one day, on their shift. Then pressure burst both his ear-drums, and he died on the spot of a brain haemorrhage.

The only thing that ever threatened Jimmy's brain was a bullet an Irish mobsman put in it, when a gang shot up a Mid-West Saloon. Unhappily, Jimmy was minding it for a pal. The gang got away with all the takings, and left Jimmy's bullet in his skull for quittance. The doctor examined Jimmy's head. Then, so Jimmy told me with simple pride, the doctor pronounced that the patient's head was very very hard, exceptionally hard, and it would be much safer to leave the bullet where it was, in view of the brute-force necessary to take it out. So there it stayed for the rest of Jimmy's life. I think he was attached to it, and proud of it, and looked upon it as a sort of Medal.

He was the toughest man for his age I have ever come across, although he was thin and small. But he was wiry, and his arms were like iron, and his fingers like steel. In my cottage walls there are some handsome granite lintels roughly four feet long and a foot square for the rest. One day he told me he'd cut dozens of them in his youth, with an axe, after his regular day's work at a quarry, and he was paid a penny each for them.

But nobody ever called Jimmy a patient man. I firmly believe that all true Cornishmen are allergic to screws. I am sure Jimmy was. I once bought some sound and seasoned timber for an inner door, and its frame, and some really good brass screws

MEVAGISSEY: " . . . smaller ports which mix business and pleasure."

GORRAN HAVEN: "... a small fishing village where I now live ... almost too ..."

THE LIZARD: ''Sometimes we would bring home a trophy of the wide ribbon seaweed, glistening with brine and water.''

NANCLEDRA: "The first village on the Concurrian, the Red River . . . Nancledra today is as lively as you make 'em."

PAINTING BY MARGO MAECKELBERGHE: "Seeing how she used storm clouds and shadows was like someone opening a previously barred door."

ZENNOR: ''The finest chunk of Cornish cliffscape? It is difficult to say . . . but this much I know it is somewhere here.''

MINACK: "We had our shield. Moments like the quiet of a Christmas morning when Jeannie and I were together, with a cat called Lama who was born within sound of the

MINACK: ''We had rejoiced in the flower season . . .''

to be used with them. To my crazed horror, I was a witness of Jimmy's ways in the use of screws. He took the first, and gave it a couple of turns with his screwdriver. Then he spat on his hands, picked up a hammer as heavy as Vulcan's and clonked the screw like a thunderbolt. I heard a sad splitting sound, as the screw violated the virgin wood.

" Proper job, Capun," said Jimmy, complacently. " I belong to fill he with cement when I'm done."

I actually ran away from him, zigzagging like a hare running from hound, and still felt like a mad March hare until I had drowned the bitter fate of my timber in bitter beer.

I was far too craven to give Jimmy a curt lecture on screwdrivers and their uses. For one thing, he would have sulked at me for weeks, and my roof was leaking near the base of a chimney-stack, and Jimmy was the supreme expert on leaks, and he had a simple discipline of no repairs for anybody whose friendship with him was in disrepair.

Then Mrs. Martin died. Jimmy seemed to have no wish to survive ; her death had stripped all pleasure from his being. Very soon after, he, too, left life behind. They were both in their late seventies. Jimmy's mother, however, survived this sterling son of hers, and lived to be 102. I saw her out walking one day, not long before her hundredth birthday. She held herself as straight as a die, and I thought what a dignified figure she cut.

Nancledra, in West Penwith — this, to me, is Cornwall ; or, in the words of the title of this book, Nancledra is " my Cornwall," and my family's too.

Before ending this, I walked down our lane to the main road. There is a honey-sweet smell of furze and wild thyme ; a soft West wind is blowing, and all the air is mild and gentle and clean.

I propose to stay at Windswept until the greatest democrat of them all calls for me to join the only silent majority that will never be outnumbered.

10

Michael Williams

Zennor

My Cornwall does not exist.

I cannot mark a spot on the map and honestly say: " This is mine!"

Maybe ancestry comes into the reckoning. My father's family came from St. Austell, from that lunar landscape belonging to the china clay industry: those white cones and the milky green-blue lakes; those dusty villages with their austere chapels and Victorian terraces. My mother's clan, in contrast, came from Penwith where you pass all the firsts and the lasts, depending whether you are going east or west: a narrow neck of land with the sea only rarely out of sight or sound. Back in time, Irish and Breton blood flowed into the family tree; little wonder then that I feel Cornish, feel distinctly Celtic, fervently believe that Cornwall is not just another English county but a people and a place apart. And as if to increase the complexity, I find myself living miles from either region, high on the jagged North Cornish coast at Bossiney, a hamlet by Tintagel, one of the old rotten boroughs which once upon a time sent not one but two Members of Parliament to London: an area haunted by the Arthurian legend, a place where it is difficult to disentangle fact from fiction, where the line dividing past and present frequently grows blurred.

My Cornwall ?

There are many images. They form themselves naturally and easily in the eye of memory or imagination — or both.

Riding across the wastes of Bodmin Moor, a weird and wonderful world of its own ; looking down from the summit of Brown Willy or Rough Tor, the sensation that you are sitting on the roof of Cornwall. Standing on the glistening black cliffs at Tintagel on a stormy day with the spray spitting in your face. Lazing on the golden sands of Daymer Bay with the sea lying like a satin lagoon. Meeting Lamorna Valley on a spring morning with daffodils splashing yellow over a green countryside ; walking along the cliff path from the cove to Carn Barges.

All these have special places in my Cornwall. These though are only pieces in the jig-saw puzzle. Perhaps they are not as I see them at all ; perhaps they are as an earthly being sees Heaven or Hell, much depending on the mood, the moment and the season.

You cannot be dogmatic about Cornwall. Shades are subtle, motives vague, strangely unsure like twilight covering a mysterious landscape or a sleeper waking from his slumber.

Death rarely arranges matters conveniently. But assuming I were allowed a last wish, were able to make a final farewell, I should have no doubt, no hesitation. There would be but one road — the road from St. Ives to Zennor.

Like Humphry Davy I was born at Penzance, lived and worked there for roughly three decades, yet I owe more to St. Ives. It was St. Ives that opened my eyes. For more than twenty years I was almost blind, seeing next to nothing, but St. Ives, and especially its art galleries, changed all that and became the window of my world. It was more than a matter of learning that art is " life-enhancing;" deeper than the discovery that a painting can enrich one's experience as can a poem or a piece of music. It was something to do with growing-up, something I never found inside a text-book during what was laughingly called my education. Without coming face to face with the sculpture, the pottery and particularly the paintings, I would have grown into a very different and certainly a poorer person. The colours and the tones, the shapes and the rhythms of Penwith, I started seeing them for the first time. It was, I think, the modern painters, rather than the older figurative artists who sharpened my perception, for when I stood on the higher ground I began to understand that Cornwall — or parts of it — sloped like a draughtsman's country.

Nowadays I never see St. Ives in summertime. Sonia and I are then too busy looking after our guests at Bossiney which is probably just as well because we hear sad stories about St. Ives in the season: cars and crowds choking the narrow streets; bodies hiding the beaches; the incessant babble of transistors; a resort getting gaudier and gaudier and everywhere the smell of fish and chips.

Miraculously though St. Ives manages an annual resurrection. As summer slips into autumn and the days shorten and the visitors dwindle to a trickle, the old town recaptures her true spirit. The harbour with boats bobbing about like bits of proverbial cork or, when the tide is out, the ribbed sand revealed and the boats lying on their sides; the quaint cottages, homes with outside stairways leading directly from the street to the first floor; that unforgettable view from the Malakoff, by the bus station, where the streets and the buildings make such fascinating patterns. They could all be taken from a novel: Fish Street, Salubrious Square, Love Lane and Virgin Street; the so-called " Island," a green hump crowned by St. Nicholas's Chapel, seen against the vast blue backcloth of the Atlantic; and, of course, St. Ives Bay, your eye easily following its graceful curve with Godrevy Lighthouse — Virginia Woolf's — away in the distance. Commercialization may have clawed but it has not destroyed. There is something not easily put into words and, at night, she assumes a different character, something more akin to the continent than Cornwall, an impression intensified if there are Breton crabbers in the bay.

I began my affair with St. Ives around my 21st birthday and I continue flirting with her between the months of November and March. She can still charm, still seduce, but spirits soar highest as I climb the Stannack, that steep hill where the miners lived — the fishermen peopled Downalong. High up on the left-hand side stands the most famous pottery in the world: Bernard Leach's. By the time you have reached the crest of the hill, the Bed & Breakfast signs have disappeared and by keeping right you meet the open country and, according to my eyes and instinct, the most magical region in all Penwith.

I never travel across this twisting Macadam without a strange sense of anticipation. The road rises and falls, straightens and curls again, snaking its way westward beneath treeless hills. To the right — and always — lies the sea. A writer can so easily overwrite, can so easily over-romanticise until his prose becomes more purple than the heather, but Zennor somehow helps you to resist the temptation ; maybe because much of this terrain is neither comfortable nor comforting. It can be cruel and wicked, like chunks lifted from Dartmoor. I have seen motorists hurrying along this road, foot hard on the accelerator, faces intent — and have wondered why. Are they like poor de la Mare? Will they too only feel safe again when they know the red soil of Devon is beneath their feet or their wheels ?

Frances Bellerby, of course, was right: "The bones of this land are not speechless." There is something savage and primitive here, eloquent perhaps yet an elusive, indefinable quality which you cannot easily pin to paper in words or on to canvas in paint. Perhaps it is best reflected in sculpture and not the sculpture of mere men. Take a look at the rocks on some of those high wind-swept spots on the left: the tors and rocking-stones and rounded basins, basins once believed to have been man-made but now known to have been shaped by Nature herself.

Those, who have eyes, will see much in this area of West Cornwall. You will, at one stage, find silhouetted against the sky a polar bear or a colossal stone formation that requires little imagination. Some say that long, long ago all the witches in Penwith assembled hereabouts at midnight on Midsummer Night, each witch lighting a fire in a rock-basin in honour of the Devil. On certain parts of Bodmin Moor and Dartmoor, I sense that the Devil himself presides, and now and then I get the same feeling here. Undeniably we have a thread of superstition in our Cornish make-up. Owing something conceivably to our Celtic ancestry? Or is it more down to earth ? Women lived in the shadow of perpetual threat: a storm at sea, an accident down a mine, events which turned wives into widows. In such environment, we may more readily accept the significance of omens, may be less cynical of the spiritual and the magical. And the complexity goes deep, for ours on the surface may. be a pagan landscape, yet basically we are an emotional, religious people. Wesley won hundreds of converts in Cornwall, but black magic too had its hold. In the Witchcraft Museum at Boscastle I have seen an interesting exhibit: a green glass bottle, "compounded by a West Cornwall Wise Woman, working in the

Ludgvan area, containing a mixture of seven herbs, human hair, shadow dust, pins and various magical powers. It was never used. The intended victim died in a road accident." And on the other side of the coin were the white witches, men and women who offered protection against the spells of Black Magic.

Zennor parish is roughly five miles in length, stretching from Morvah in the west to Towednack in the east. Northward is the open ocean and facing it some of the finest cliffs in Britain: a mixture of granite and greenstone. Inland lies a shelf, and southward, from approximately the 400 feet contour, the ground leaps dramatically, doubling its height, to a backbone ridge and plateau. Men and women have toiled at agriculture in these parts since the Middle and Late Bronze Ages, and agriculture remains important today. Though tourism has exploded in Cornwall, Zennor thankfully, incredibly, is virtually untouched, unscarred, little changed, in fact, from days when the sails of Phoenician galleys fluttered off the Cornish coast.

Even the cottages and the farm houses have a certain solidity, some giving the impression that they have grown out of the landscape. Many modern constructions, in comparison, look flimsy and temporal. Zennor's most imposing residence is Eagle's Nest, standing on the seaward side of the B3306; a large Victorian house, built at 621 feet on a granite outcrop, it is the home of Patrick Heron, the painter. Next door is the Old Poor House and another painter, Alethea Garstin, daughter of Norman Garstin, who was a pioneer in Newlyn's creation as an artists' colony, and whose brother Crosbie was the well-known Westcountry novelist.

Opposite the two houses, a path, meandering through the bracken, climbs towards Zennor Quoit. Invisible from the road but less than a mile away as the crow supposedly flies, it is well worth the deviation. Even in its present ruined condition — due to the vandalism of a Georgian farmer — Zennor Quoit remains a noble monument. Somebody has said that in Penwith you find yourself walking among " the early instalments of history." I certainly feel so when I come face to face with this great battered dolmen. Time appears to contract, and as when I meet a Barbara Hepworth sculpture there is the temptation to handle and, in the moment of physical contact, a notion that somehow, in some strange way, one is in touch with a distant power. Belonging to the Megalithic Age — the great stone period — Zennor Quoit can only be vaguely dated as somewhere between

2000 and 1500 B.C. Bodies of the dead were laid here. Zennor and Trethevy by St. Cleer, up at the other end of the county, are the only Cornish quoits with a brace of chambers. Time was when Zennor had seven side-slabs and terminals. But the huge flat capstone has been wrenched from its supports and is now propped against them. Theory has it that a local farmer wanted to use the stones for cattle shelters and one can only guess that he erected the four stone posts nearby.

Also nearby are a cottage and studio belonging to Margo Maeckelberghe, the Penzance painter. Margo Maeckelberghe's name — for me anyway — conjures up a picture of Penwith: images of Cornish land and seascapes, storm scarred skies and seas to match, majestic moorland and headlands thrusting their craggy faces into the Atlantic, sloping fields and solitary cottages. She is Cornish yet cosmopolitan. Like the late Peter Lanyon, Margo Maeckelberghe is a native, an insider looking out, and like Lanyon she has travelled — Belgium and Spain, Italy and Greece — she has gone beyond a purely Cornish context, yet her anchorage remains firmly here in West Cornwall. Back at Bossiney we feel we can always slip back to Penwith in spirit because we have several of her paintings. Our dining room is dominated by her *Sea Spate*, a large oil beautifully but menacingly reflecting the never-ending struggle between the North Cornish coast and the Atlantic, the blue suddenly, dramatically turning into white foam.

Margo maintains the light of Penwith is both the magnet and the key for the painter: " This crystal-clear light . . . it gives everything a new meaning ; the form and the structure of the landscape is defined and enlarged by it. The landscape itself is interesting, but the light does something to it." She also believes "creativity breeds creativity . . . but I get the impression that it's more difficult for a Cornish man or woman to enter the world of Cornish painting than somebody who comes in from outside. You're there, yet you're not there. Everybody else has this romantic concept of Cornwall, but if you're here, if you're related to the people and the place, you know it's not romantic and you see it quite differently. Ben Nicholson, I am certain, was one outsider who understood this. You get this mathematical, draughtsmanlike quality about his Cornish painting. I believe mathematics are essential to art ; they're allied. The artist measures with his eye ; the mathematician with his rule."

Personally I shall always be grateful to her for torpedoing the nonsense we talk about " bad weather." Seeing how she used storm clouds and shadows was like someone opening a previously barred door. Even a painting of Cornwall in the heat of summer can somehow strangely hold a threat, clouds casting shadows hinting at the possibility of storm. Later — much later — I stood before the Turners in the Tate and saw how the greatest of British painters transformed wind and rain and storm into sheer masterpieces. Weather forecasts ceased to deter and a grey misty morning suddenly added a new dimension.

I am also deeply grateful to Charles Simpson, the painter and writer. He was one of the last links with what some would call the golden age of Cornish painting, he was born in 1894, the Webbs were creating the Fabian Society and Pasteur was experimenting with something called innoculation. I don't think the younger generation realized how highly he had been regarded. Guy Paget rated him: " the greatest bird painter living." Charles Simpson, would however have nothing to do with modern trends in art, loathed the term realistic: " I prefer to say I belong to the conservative school or, if you like, the real painters!"

It was though, I think, his conversation and his writing that helped me most. We spent happy hours in that spacious room upstairs at Stanley House, Penzance, facing Mount's Bay. He had a descriptive talent which some likened to Hudson and he loved this coastline: " the northern cliffs frown upon the sea, an unbroken barrier of rock, grey as the jackdaw's mantle, sombre as the raven's wing." He helped me to understand the magic of moorland, especially its peculiar power in the hour between sunset and darkness. ". . . when ponies wander freely, foxes bark, animals call and only man wants to hide."

Thanks to Charles Simpson, I started walking across Hannibal's Carn with fresh vision. I began to detect the shades and the subtleties of Penwith's landscape, the bracken, for example, changing from the green of summer to the " swarthy, smouldering red of autumn." I began to enjoy poking about in the past, though perhaps enjoy is the wrong verb, for often I felt a spirit of awe. " Tracing the history of these relics," he once put it, " is like reading a book whose pages grow blurred and confused as the plot unfolds." And relics can mean anything from a deserted ivy-coated cottage with crumbling masonry to some famous ancient monument. Bosporthennis, by the way, two miles south-west of Zennor Churchtown is an iron age village. One house, said to be over 2,000 years old, is roofed with overlapping courses of masonry like an Irish beehive. Anyone exploring Zennor or any part of Penwith for that matter needs an Ordnance Map ; and those who restrict themselves to a motor car and the main roads will miss most.

Writers and artists of all breeds have been drawn to this most westerly peninsula. Penwith has probably attracted more than any other Cornish region ; maybe the sheer extremity has had something to do with it, the realization that you can go no further, that the Land's End is literal, or possibly writers have the habit of following famous footsteps. Anyway D. H. Lawrence lived here at Zennor for a while, at Tregerthen, a tiny cottage, by a rough track down a dip below Eagle's Nest and the Old Poor House. It faces fields divided by stone walls, fields with the occasional stones looking like some cabbage that has grown out of the soil and gone wrong ; and beyond the fields are the cliffs and the ocean. There were only two rooms, one up and one down with a long scullery, but the rent was modest enough: a mere four shillings a week. "It is not England," Lawrence reflected. "It is bare and elemental, Tristan's land. I lie looking down at a cove where the waves come white under a low, black headland which slopes up in bare green-brown, bare and sad under a level sky. It is old, Celtic, pre-Christian." And later he wrote: "It is a cove like Tristian sailed into, from Lyonesse — just the same. It belongs to 2,000 years back — that pre-Arthurian Celtic flicker of being which has disappeared so entirely . . . All is desolate and forsaken, not linked up. But I like it."

Tregerthen however was no idyllic episode for Lawrence. The Murrys left him and went to Mylor. He was wounded and his comments bitter: "Unfortunately the Murrys do not like the country — it is too rocky and bleak for them. They should have a soft valley with leaves and the ringdove cooing. And this is a hillside of rocks and magpies and foxes."

Earlier at Portcothan he had been caustic too about the Cornish, likening them to "insects." At Zennor he thought them "decent" but eventually had reason to amend that view. Any village in Cornwall — or England — in 1917 would have been suspicious of a man with a German wife, especially one with a proud repertoire of German songs, and Zennor, with the Great

War raging, was no exception. First, there were accusations of disobedience during the black-out and lights signalling out to sea. Then the Lawrence mail was withheld and scrutinised ; later soldiers searched the cottage and finally the author and his wife were ordered to leave Cornwall within three days without explanation. "Desolate and forsaken," had been prophetic words.

The same stairs that Lawrence climbed are still in the cottage ; the kitchen shelves are reputed to have been made by Lawrence himself. I have climbed the stairs and looked northward, to the sea, from the window in his bedroom and have felt sad. Surely he never forgave us.

In and around Zennor I find myself meeting myself — not the face in this morning's mirror but recalling events that belong to the past, encountering a stranger who bears an identical name. Exploring this region — in the memory — brings the terrible realization that few friendships, only rare relationships, stand the test of time ; not merely a matter of drifting apart but the result of circumstances or the thing we call Fate. Could one pick up the threads? One will probably never know.

Playing against Zennor at cricket on a Sunday in a field by the Gurnard's Head Hotel — I can almost hear my leg stump being flattened by a quick, low delivery from a round-arm bowler ; seeing my first fox, a beautiful creature, gliding across a patch of green, then disappearing into coppery bracken ; spending half a foggy evening trying to find the inn at Zennor and ending up drinking miles away at St. Just ; meeting Zennor Church and the Mermaid for the first time ; spending an afternoon arguing with a friend about something that didn't really matter and never seeing him again — all these stand out with diamond sharpness. Strangely enough looking back on my life I can see now that some of my most important decisions have been made at Zennor. The long, alleged arm of coincidence? Or did I deliberately go out there? I don't know. Possibly I should have kept a Zennor diary, for searching our memories can be a sad, almost frightening experience when we discover how little we retain.

Zennor itself is a small village, seemingly halting the wild moors as they come tumbling down to the fantastic cliffs. An Inn, The Tinners Arms, a cluster of cottages, a church and a chapel, there is little else. Hamlet really is the word.

There may be more beautiful, more historic churches than Zennor's St. Senara, but, for me, it has a special atmosphere and charm. I shall never forget seeing it for the first time, decorated for Easter Day. Perhaps though the truth is that, as a small boy, I fell in love with the Mermaid of Zennor. I certainly still love the legend.

Once upon a time — as all good stories should begin — a beautiful and elegantly dressed lady attended occasional services at Zennor church. Although the Cornish have a bush telegraph system which outmatches anything produced by the G.P.O., this lady remained a mystery. Nobody knew her name or address ; nobody knew anything about her, but young Mathey Trewella, the squire's son, a handsome lad with one of the finest voices in the parish, resolved to solve the mystery. He, like half the male population, had probably fallen for her, so one Sunday evening after the service he followed her down to the cliffs. Neither were seen again. Years later a ship cast anchor in Pendour Cove when suddenly the captain heard a beautiful voice hailing him from the waters below. It was a Mermaid with long strands of blonde hair floating around her body who politely asked him to shift his vessel as its anchor was blocking the entrance to her home under the sea and she wanted to get back to her husband Mathey and their children. A very frightened captain returned to Zennor with the tale — seamen always associate Mermaids with bad luck — and after much discussion it was decided to put the Mermaid of Zennor in the church as a warning to young men against the wiles of Mermaids.

And there she is today, an exquisitely carved figure on a bench end, mirror in one hand, comb in the other, long hair cascading over her shoulders. Local people used to say that if you listened carefully on a moonlight night you could hear her singing, but I've never been that lucky. I have come on a night when the moon made an oily ocean and Pendeen Lighthouse winked its regular patterns, but all I heard was the music of the waves.

At least I have Christine Quayle's lovely young voice on the *Sounds like West Cornwall* record. Christine apparently came to live on the site of Mathey's old home, felt compelled to sing and became known professionally as the Mermaid of Zennor. The song recorded, *The Seagulls Scream*, she actually composed on the cliffs here at Zennor.

Buildings are not dumb. Most old ones have something to say, provided we have the humility to keep quiet and listen. As for churches, some, by my reckoning, have a doomed air, almost as if they are contradicting the optimism of the New Testament and a belief in the resurrection. Others have a warmth and a welcome. Here at Zennor I come out into the open air with a lighter steps. Churchyards too make an impact. I find myself standing in some staring at the headstones: "Gone but not forgotten" are the sentiments yet feeling that somebody is lying, and that feeling stems from an ingredient deeper than long grass, weeds and dead flowers. But at Zennor I am convinced the grave is not the end, that death is only a doorway, admittedly leading to somewhere we know little or nothing about.

On the church tower, which dominates the whole village-scape, is a slate sun-dial, dated 1737, and below it is a stone to "John Davey (1812-1891) of Boswednack in this parish . . . who was the last to possess any traditional considerable knowledge of the Cornish language:" words which dent old Dolly Pentreath's reputation. Dolly, who liver over at Mousehole by St. Clement's Isles on the rim of Mount's Bay and who claimed to be the last native speaker, passed on before John Davey was born! However nobody denies the fact that Mousehole — pronounced Mou'zl — was one of the last strongholds of the Cornish language or that Dolly remains a formidable character in Cornish history. It was Dolly's custom to beg for coins, jabbering away in the Cornish language, and when no coins were forthcoming she unleashed a barrage of curses. There is an obelisk, surmounted by a cross, to Dolly in Paul churchyard. One of the sponsors of the stone was Prince Louis Lucien Bonaparte, a keen student of languages.

Happily, character and individuality — or a measure of these qualities — still flourish in Cornwall. It is not surprising John Wesley did well here ; we are essentially non-conformists. Our fish man, for instance, firmly declines to go decimal, you still get your prices in the old coin language. There is a cottage, not far from where I live, which boldly displays the following notice: "This property is not for sale." And I was told of a certain Cornish farmer who, when it rains, sheds his shirt, jacket and trousers and proceeds to operate his tractor in only vest and underpants. I have met an Irishman wandering on the cliffs, early one morning: "looking for me false teeth, mister," and I have seen "hippies" frying their breakfast of bacon and eggs over a grave in a churchyard. Cornwall, as I said earlier, is a place and a people apart, and funnily enough some of the 'furriners' become more Cornish than the Cornish.

Up the road, beyond the Wayside Museum, is a stone from which John Wesley preached. Another interesting stone is the Giant's, in the opposite direction, roughly two furlongs north of the church. This 22 feet long stone, resting on another, is said to be a logen, but I doubt if even Hercules himself could persuade this one to log.

Though normally reluctant to recommend places — people's palates vary on everything, one man's meat and all that — I have however no hesitation about recommending The Tinner's Arms ; convivial evenings spent there shape themselves naturally in recollection.* The inn takes its name from the days when the mines were living things ; mining company board meetings were help upstairs with dinner invariably following business discussion.

Not all tourist amenities and so-called attractions add dignity to our county. One thinks sadly of the hordes of caravans and chalets, and all those gift shops with shoddy products from Hong Kong, but Zennor, happily offers something essentially Cornish and authentic. Up the road from The Tinner's Arms, just below Wesley's stone is the Wayside Museum. Domestic implements like box irons and scrowling irons for grilling pilchards, kettles and baking plates ; agricultural implements such as ploughs and tommyhawks, barley prongs and dung forks ; quarry tools, hammers and axes, jumpers for drilling holes (five feet long), and feathers and wedge for rock splitting ; bits and pieces from the days of the fishing fleets: net needles of wood and bone, the fisherman's butter horn and the limpet crook — everything was made or used in Cornwall. The open hearth in the cottage alone is worth a visit. The creator of this richly diverse collection was the late Colonel Hirst who, one day before the 1939 war, standing on Hayle Quay and studying a hillock of scrap-metal bound for Germany, noted how many strange tools and implements lay there. Before long the Colonel's curiosity had turned into a search among the old barns and mowhays and the collection had begun.

Inevitably though — for me — any journey's end must be on the Zennor coastline, upon rough granite walls where the cliffs and the Atlantic battle unceasingly.

The finest chunk of Cornish cliffscape? It's difficult to say, after all this coastline of ours is longer than any English county — a length of 245 miles — but this much I know it is somewhere

* I remember too catching the landlord in that Sunday cricket match, it's strange how cricketers accurately record the catches they took, but never the chances they missed.

here. Some would say the Horse's Back on Zennor Head ; others would say Porthglaze Pinnacles or Gurnard's Head, probably the most famous of the lot. Our eyes are said to be the windows of our souls, I believe these cliffs then are the Cornish windows. Come here anytime and in any weather and you will see what I mean. If driven to make a choice, it would, on reflection, be Zennor Head, preferably on a stormy day when hundreds of white horses come careering home on an angry, heaving sea, reminding me of the lost land of Lyonesse and the one man who survived riding a grey horse.

Who knows, like Mathey Trewella, who came out onto these cliffs long, long ago, maybe I too am trying to unravel a mystery.

11

Derek Tangye

Minack

We stood outside the cottage and stared ; Hans Andersen cottage with the primitive beauty of a crofter's home, sad and neglected as if it were one of the grey boulders in the wild land around. The walls seemed to grow out of the ground, great rocks fingering up the sides until they met the man placed stones, rough faced granite slabs bound together by clay. Once upon a time, it appeared to us, there might have been upstairs rooms and perhaps a roof of thatch ; but now the roof was an uncouth corrugated iron jagged with holes, tilting so steeply that it resembled a man's cap pulled over his eyes ; and prodding defiantly into the sky above it, as if ashamed of being associated with such ugliness, was a massive lichen-covered chimney. The poky windows peered from the darkness within, three facing the moorland and the sea, and two either side of the battered door which looked upon the unkempt once loved tiny garden. We pushed the door and it was unlocked. Wooden boards peppered with holes gnawed by rats covered the floor, and putting my hand through one of them I touched the wet earth. The walls were mustard yellow with old paper and though the area of the cottage was that of an old fashioned drawing-room it was divided into four rooms, matchbox thick divisions yielding the effect of privacy. At right angles to the door in a cavity of the wall beneath the chimney, an ancient Cornish range seared with rust, droppings of rats dirtying the oven, brandished the memories of forgotten meals. Above, the sagging thin boards of the ceiling drooped in curves, rimmed grey in patches from rain dripping through the roof. A cupboard faced the door and inside broken crockery lay on the shelves, a brown kettle without a lid, and a mug imprinted with a coloured picture of King George V and Queen Mary side by side. Musty with long absence of an inhabitant, lugubrious with the crush of the toy sized rooms, the cottage seemed yet to shine with welcome ; and we felt as if we had entered Aladdin's Cave.

Outside we stood by the corner of the cottage, the battered door facing climbing ground behind us, and looked down upon a shadow of a valley, gentle slopes, heading for the sea. Beyond was the Carn where we had stood, cascading below it a formation of rocks resembling an ancient castle, and in the distance across the blue carpet of sea the thin white line of breakers dashing against the shores of Prah Sands, Porthleven and Mullion. A lane drifted away from the cottage. On its right was a barn with feet thick walls in which were open slits instead of windows and on its left was a tumbled-down stone hedge, holding back the woods we had seen and the jungle-like growth, as policemen try to hold back a bursting throng. The lane led down to a stream, dammed into a pool by the density of the weeds which blocked its outflow, and then, a few yards on, petered out in a tangle of brushwood and gorse bushes. We could see that the cottage was only connected with civilisation by a track through a field.

We had changed since we had first known each other, Jeannie and I. Once we had both fought hard to savour flattery and power, to be part of a glad world of revelry, to be in the fashion, and to rush every day at such speed that we disallowed ourselves any opportunity to ponder where we were going. It is easy to remain in a groove, a groove which becomes worn without you realising it, only recognisable by friends who have not seen you for a long time, and it is usually luck which enables you to escape. Jeannie and I had the luck to feel the same at the same time, and so we had been united in forcing ourselves to flee our conventional background. There had never been any argument between us about the pros and cons, gradually the standards we once believed so important appeared sadly ineffectual, only vital until they had been experienced. Moreover the merciless zest required to achieve them became an exhausting effort as soon as the standards, reached at last, had to be maintained; for it became obvious to us that in most cases the banners of success were made of paper, waved by entrepreneurs who were temporarily leeching on the creative efforts of others.

Thus Jeannie and I belonged to the lucky ones who, having seen their personal horizon, had also reached it ; and yet in doing so there was no possible reason for self satisfaction. It was true that contentment was always near us, but there was an edge to our life which stopped us from ever taking it for granted. What had become our strength was the base to which we could retreat. We had a home we loved. Around us was the ambience of permanency. We had roots. And so, when we became involved in sophisticated stresses which touched us with memories of other days, there was a moat behind which we could recharge. We then could observe quietly the enemy ; envy, for instance, the most corroding of sins, the game of intrigue which fills so many people's lives, the use of the lie which in business is considered a justifiable weapon, the hurt that comes from insecurity, the greed which feeds on itself, the worship of headline power without quality to achieve it. We watched, and sometimes we were vexed, sometimes we were frightened. Across the moat we could see the reflections of the past.

The Minack meadows had been the first to be planted and thus the first to be peppered with green but the Pentewan meadows, aided by the extra hour of the sun they received as they stared south towards the Wolf Rock, were quick to catch up. Soon, in the mild weather, the plants were growing so fast that the pundits were talking of the earliest potato season on record ; and Jeannie and I rejoiced that it seemed we were scheduled for beginner's luck. John was happy enough to smile and volunteer good mornings, and Joe's boss — the farmer who rented us Pentewan — forgot his quiet self and made jokes. There was a pleasant camaraderie on the cliffs, and confidence that all would share unenviously in the prosperity ahead.

One afternoon, it was Thursday March 27th, we heard a chiff-chaff making its monotonous call, the first of the year, the wonder of its African journey transferred to Minack woods :

and it gave us the cool pleasure of confidence in ourselves and our surroundings. The cry followed us: 'Chiff Chaff! Chiff Chaff!' — and the sound of its limited note, amid trees pinking with buds, moss brightening with growth on old rocks, primroses a secret ecstasy unless unexpectedly discovered, pools of ragged robin and blue-bells . . . the sound of its limited note derided the tyranny of the automaton age and the warped values that advance the putrid aims of the dodgers of truth, the cynical commentators of the passing scene, the purveyors of mass inertia. The dull two notes of the tiny bird trumpeted defiance of the fake and the slick, bringing to the shadows in the woods the expanse of its own achievement ; until the sound gently entered the evening, and as night fell, hid among the trees.

It was suddenly cold, and as I came back from shutting up the chickens a sudden breeze hit the branches above my head, a sharp thrust from the east. Indoors Jeannie was stirring soup on the stove while Monty was behaving as if scissors were after his tail and dinosaurs awaiting his pounce.

'What on earth's wrong with Monty tonight ?' And I bent down and tried to pick him up. He darted to the door and when I moved to open it, rushed to the sofa, forking his claws in the side, raking the material, and earning a 'Shut up, Monty!' from Jeannie. There was a sound outside as if a car was driving up to the cottage. 'Listen,' I said, and we paused, tense. 'It's a plane,' said Jeannie, relieved. There it was again, a rushing, moaning sound. 'It isn't,' I answered knowledgeably, 'it's the wind.'

It was the sound of the scouts, the fingers of the wind, stretching ahead probing the hills and woods, the rocks and hedges, the old cottages, the lonely trees acting as sentinels of the land. They probe and jab, searching for flying leaves, decaying branches ready to fall, for flowers youthfully in bloom, for the green swath of the potato tops ; and finding, they rush on searching for more, magnificently confident that the majesty of the gale which follows will crush and pound and obliterate. And when they have gone there is an instant of stillness to remind you of a quiet evening, the passing assurance of a safe world, and you wait ; you wait and wonder if you were wrong and the wind is innocent ; you listen, your mind peeling across the green meadows whose defences are impotent ; then suddenly the slap of the face and the braying of hounds of hell and the heaving mountain of maniacal power.

The gale roared without pause till the afternoon of March 29th, vicious, friendless and with frost in its scream; here was man as helpless as the foam on the rocks, centuries of rising conceit contemptuously humbled, the joke of the tempest. Action was masochistic. We struggled heads down as if fighting a way through invisible jungle grass, buffeted, pushed back, soundless in our shouting, kneeling to the ground to gape at a meadow in its progress towards obliteration, then hustled home as if our coats were kites, running without effort, feathers in air.

We sat and waited. The vapid wait, droning the hours away with our fears, calculating losses, listening to the ships' waveband as vessels neared Land's End ('I don't fancy going round the corner'), unknown voices sharing our company, leaping to the window when the noise for a second abated, hearing the sea hissing like a coastline of cobras, sleeping with demons in our dreams. Waiting, waiting, waiting. And when it was over, when our ears were still humming with the beating drums of fury and the sea still heaved in mud-grey valleys, we went out into an afternoon that had suddenly become as caressing as a summer's day; as if a lost temper had been replaced by shame and the cost of havoc was being guiltily assessed.

The Minack meadows were a pattern of black stumps; in pocket-sized havens the wind had entered like a tornado, and there were gaps where not even stumps were to be seen. At Pentewan the army of green, the plants the size of cabbages had become a foot-high petrified forest drooping in the sunshine like melting black candles. Black also was the grass on the banks, filmed as if with tar, and the stinging nettles which once taunted us to scythe them down; and here and there wild daffodils stared forlornly with petals shredded into tea-stained strips; or with necks broken, their heads drooped against the stems like victims of the gallows. The desolation looked up at the blue sky and the fleck of a lark singing. A magpie flew by coarsely chattering, and for a second I saw a fox silhouetted on a rock above the quarry. A boat chugged by outward bound to the fishing grounds beyond the Isles of Scilly, and we looked down at the men on deck as if we were on a hill and they in a valley. Normality was returning even if the thrash of the whip was still in our ears; ideas began to form, the warm challenge born of disaster quickened our minds, the sense of comradeship which frays in tedious defeat but sharpens in sudden defeat, became exhilarated, and I greeted Joe as if victory was our companion.

★

The village of St. Buryan is three miles away from us, and it is a sturdy village which has an atmosphere that suggests it has an inbred awareness of its past. Historically it dates back to the sixth century when an Irish girl saint called Berian travelled this way and founded a shrine in the then encampment ; and later in the tenth century King Athelstan, after defeating the Danes at Boleigh Hill, worshipped at the shrine before setting out with his army from the beaches of Sennen to drive the Danes from the Scilly Isles. He made a vow, when he was at the shrine that he would endow and build a church at St. Buryan if the expedition was successful. He kept his vow, and the original church lasted until the fifteenth century ; then the present one was built, a beautiful building with a fine tower which in the days of sail was a landmark for ships far out to sea. Yet it is not just the historical aspect which gives St. Buryan its strength. This is a village which has belonged so much to the soil, the storms, the droughts, the daily struggle of living with nature over the centuries that the villagers whose families have lived here for generations are instinctively loyal to the basic values. They hold firm opinions, are kind. and generous, but are never strident. Outsiders are now coming to live in the village, and whereas five years ago there were only solid granite cottages to live in, one now sees on the outskirts an increasing number of bungalows with outside walls faced with ersatz stone. Old men, sitting on the bench in front of the church, see someone go by and do not know their name ; old men on the same bench a few years ago knew the intimate personal story of everyone they saw.

We buy our weekly groceries at St. Buryan from the shop which is simply called the Shop. ('I'm going up shop' say the locals). It is run by a couple called Lily and Ted Chapple who offer that personal service to their customers that a computer might tell them was uneconomic. They know the special whims and fancies of all who come to them, young and old ; and at Christmas time they follow a custom that the computer would certainly condemn. Each regular customer receives a present, and a handsome one at that. The Shop is indeed in tune with the character of St. Buryan, though it now has to compete with a flush of supermarkets that national chains have introduced into Penzance after buying up old fashioned concerns. Tempting advertisements, promising twopence off this and fourpence off that, try to lure the ladies of St. Buryan to transfer their allegiance from the Shop to Penzance. There is, however, the bus fare to be paid ; and the personal attention to be lost.

Across the road from the Shop are the pub and the Post Office. We used to go regularly to the pub in the days of the landlord called Jim Grenfell ; and ten years ago before the mains were brought to the village, I used to stand at the bar window watching the villagers queueing up with their pails to collect water from the village well opposite. The pub has now been redesigned, and the present landlord is known as one of the most welcoming in West Cornwall, but we seldom go there ourselves. There is no fun now in going to the village pub if you live outside the village. Instead of having a roistering time, there you are standing by the bar clinically deciding whether the law will allow you another half pint. Maybe it is a worthy law but it is a law that has resulted in the loss of a legion of friendships. And the teetotallers drive as fast as ever.

The Post Office is presided over by Leslie Payne, a kind man whose occasional vagueness endears him to the many who appreciate his gentle character. His courtesy is famous and if you are engaged in some post office business, you may find yourself being offered a sweet from a large tin. He takes infinite trouble with any inquiry and, if you are accustomed to some city post offices, you will regret that Leslie Payne is not your local postmaster. He also sells fruit and vegetables, sweets and a few groceries and also newspapers. We have our Sunday newspapers from him, but he does not have a high opinion of newspapers. 'Another load of rubbish,' he will say as he hands the bundle over to us. Or during the week he may hand us, instead of the paper of the day, an out-of-date issue saying we will not notice the difference.

'I've a fine crop of lettuces,' I would say to Jacksons, 'how many would you like ?'

Having pursued the struggle of growing them and having poured out the cost, a grower when asking this question is in the same mood as a prima donna before an opera performance. He is tensed.

' How many ?'

' Oh well,' comes the answer, ' the public are not buying lettuce. Say ten dozen.'

Jeannie and I have spent many hours of our lives standing in the forecourt of Jacksons store on the front at Penzance discussing lettuces with Fred the foreman or one of the Jackson brothers.

' Surely you can take more than ten dozen ?'

' We can't sell what we've got, old man. Honest we can't.'

' I've run out of crates, Fred.'

' Hang on a moment, I'll get you some.'

' When shall I come again ?'

' Make it Friday, early as possible, old man.'

This is the tedious part of growing. The part I do not envisage when the seeds are sown; then all my hopes and concern and endeavour dwell on the struggle to produce the crop. I am blind to the time when I have to sell, when the results of all the hard work depend on the unpredictable whim of the public. My cocoon of pleasure that is wrapped around the achievement of growing a fine crop is now torn to shreds. I am back again in the metallic world from which I sought to escape. I must be a businessman, and bargain and argue and flatter ; and I must be prepared to face the fact that what has been produced is not wanted.

And then, perhaps the day I have returned to Jeannie in gloom, I get a message from Jacksons: ' Bring in as many lettuces as you can.' The public, overnight, have acquired a taste for lettuce. A miraculous force has gathered them together and marched them to the greengrocers. Nothing rational about it. Nothing that even the most experienced could foresee. Just a whim.

Sometimes on these summer mornings when the Jackson order was a big one, Shelagh would come in early too. And there were occasions when Julius would also proudly arrive.

' A record walk this morning. Clipped a minute off my time.'

His was a wonderful walk. He was sleeping in a caravan in the woods of an estate a couple of miles away ; and the route to Minack was across green fields that were raised like a plateau above the sea, then down into a valley where a stream rushed in haste, leaping the boulders, sheltered by a wood where foxes hid, bordered by lush vegetation in summer, and in winter welcoming snipe and woodcock giving them a home safe from the guns. Julius loved this walk. He crossed the valley, then up past Jane's cottage and over the stone hedges to Minack.

'Heavens, Julius, I didn't expect to see you today.'

'I thought I might be able to help.'

He would always quickly go and have a look at Boris the drake because, I believe, he was proud that he had named him. There was, for always, a link between the two. It may not have been very important, but then I sometimes wonder how to gauge the degrees of importance. I have remembered many things, which at the time outsiders would have considered insignificant.

Julius was one of those people who, youthful though they may be, instinctively wish to help others. It is not just the question of intuition when to continue a line of thought, or when to stop. There are no lessons to be given about these things ; the sense of embarrassment which for a second may be hinted, or the flicker in eyes which give a clue to secret hurt, or the flavour of a moment which insists on a change of subject, none of these occasions can be dealt with by rule of thumb. Instinct is the king.

Thus Jeannie and I would be there with these three who had the promise of the years before them, each helping us, each so full of secret thoughts and hopes, puzzled, contradictory, timid and brave, obstinate and imaginative. I understood why Jeannie said to me one day that she was grateful for the necessity of cutting lettuces ; a humble task, perhaps, but there was more to gain than the price received.

The promise of the years . . . how strange it was, in view of what was to happen, that it should be Shelagh living now in the same caravan a year later, who told us that Julius had died in a motor accident.

★

When they came he could have been excused if Fred had been startled by their number. He had never seen so many children before, so many gay, shouting children who tumbled out of cars, running up the path to the field, calling: 'Happy birthday, Freddie!' This was a carnival of a party, a boy was

131

dressed as the Mad Hatter, battered top hat and tails too big for him, another wore a huge mask of the March Hare, girls in party frocks with ribbons in their hair, boys chasing each other, all converging on Fred who stood his ground half-way up the slope of the field with ears pricked ; and I would have forgiven him if he had turned and fled. Thirty-two children swarming towards him, screams of laughter, yells of glee, this cacophony of happiness made noise enough to scare him into leaping into the next field. He did not budge. He awaited the onslaught of arms being flung around him, ears pulled, mane ruffled, nose kissed and kissed again, pats on the back, tail tugged, as if it were an experience to which he had long been accustomed. All through the afternoon he allowed himself to be treated as a toy, and not once did he show impatience. Dear one-year-old Fred. This was indeed his hour of glory.

There were rewards, of course. His guests, for instance, vied with each other in their generosity, eating part of their ice-cream cornets then pushing them towards a large, welcoming mouth. He had always loved ice-cream. And there were the sticky lollipops, the shape and colour of carrots which Jeannie had bought ; and these too were dangled before him in such a way that when accepted, kudos was obtained.

Penny, meanwhile, was having her own passage of fame. Fred, being too young to carry anyone, Penny had to play the role of the patient beach donkey. Can I have a ride? Can I? Can I? Up and down the field she went, solemnly and safely. Sometimes two astride her back, sometimes even three. She plodded on in the manner of a donkey who knew how to earn its living. She waited quietly as someone was heaved upon her back, she moved at the right moment, she halted as soon as a fair ride had been completed. Can I have a ride? Can I? Can I?

There they were, two donkeys with ice-cream smeared about their faces, sucking lollipops ; Fred a toy donkey, Penny a working one, when the time came for The Cake. Jeannie had made it, a table on the field was ready for it, and there was a single candle.

The air was still, and with ceremony the candle was lit. The table was at the bottom of the field above the wood and so its shelter helped the flame to burn steadily and with no fear of it flickering out. All around were Fred's guests. There was chattering and laughter, and from somewhere in the background a small voice began the customary birthday song.

' Too soon!' someone else shouted.

Fred, at that moment, had not arrived. He was a few yards away in a cluster of admirers, a girl with golden hair holding the halter, and all of them edging Fred towards the climax of his party. He did not want to be rushed. He was going to arrive in his own good time. And suddenly the shouts went up: ' Here's Freddie! Happy birthday, Freddie! Good old Freddie!' Treble voices sailing into the sky. A moment in time that many years away, most would remember. Nothing complicated. The same pleasure that centuries have enjoyed.

Fred reached the table. The candle on the cake, a strong, confident flame, awaited him. But I do not think anyone who was present believed he would so successfully fulfil their secret hopes.

As the children sang his birthday song, Fred pushed his head forward inquiringly towards the candle, snorted ; and blew it out.

Sophie, George Brown's wife, lunched with us the day of the party which had brought us to London, and I am glad she did. Jeannie had bought a little black dress with a wide white collar from some boutique, and when she tried it on I said I didn't like it. So when Sophie arrived, Jeannie immediately asked for her aid ; she put the dress on again and Sophie was full of praise, and I found myself liking the dress after all. Sophie has that kind, comfortable manner which makes you believe she is right.

The party was to begin at six o'clock and it was being held on the sixteenth floor of New Zealand House in the Haymarket. The object was to celebrate the selection by Hatchards of the top twenty Authors of the Year ; and ' A Donkey In The Meadow ' had won me a place among them. But as the party drew near I had a queer sense of sadness, as if I were remembering all my other selves whose morale at the time would have been boosted, had they been able to foresee such an occasion.

At 5 p.m. A. P. Herbert arrived in our suite. He was one of the special guests and we had agreed that the three of us would go together. This kind, humble, marvellous original had shared with us many gay moments. The continuous achievement of his life has been to protest with wit but without malice. He has this wonderful gift of debunking humbug, and he does this without any wish for personal showmanship. I suppose his philosophy is that everyone should have fun, but it should never be fun at somebody else's expense . . . unless the somebody is a kill-joy. He has never created, artificially, subjects and matters to attack. Wit, for him, has never been a commercial commodity. He waits until injustice arouses him.

The three of us stood at the window of the sitting room looking down on the necklace of car lights passing along the embankment. On the other side of the river the windows of the Shell building popped one by one into darkness as the staff set out for home. On our right, beyond the trains of Hungerford Bridge, was the Lantern Light of the Big Ben Tower . . . the lantern is always lit while the House of Commons is sitting. Below us on the river, the tide full, were the tugs and their barges, port lights and starboard lights, and as we watched them Alan Herbert started to sing a song from the musical play he wrote with Vivian Ellis soon after the war, called ' *Big Ben.*'

London Town is built on London River

And London River flows sixty miles to sea.

He finished a verse, and started to sing it again. It was a moving moment listening to him, and funny too. He didn't take his voice very seriously. And when he finished the verse for the second time, I said he ought to persuade someone to put on a festival of Herbert musical plays. ' *Derby Day,*' ' *Tantivy Towers,*' ' *Helen,*' ' *Big Ben,*' ' *Bless The Bride,*' ' *Tough At The Top,*' ' *The Water Gypsies.*' It was a good list.

' Meanwhile,' I said, ' it's time to go.'

We went along the corridor to the lift, and soon we were in the hall waiting for the taxi which the porter was calling for us. Alan went over to the florist kiosk which stands by the revolving doors. And when he came back, he held out to Jeannie two tiny pink orchids. They looked perfect on her dress.

' Your taxi is here, sir,' said the porter.

A quarter of an hour later I was gazing at the twenty books of the year ; and in the middle was ' *A Donkey In The Meadow* ' with its picture of Fred as a foal on the jacket. And I suddenly longed for Minack.

'Jeannie,' I said, as the two of us looked at it, 'within forty-eight hours we'll be back.'

★

The only entrance to our cliff was through this gate at the top. It was no place for strangers. There was a deep cleft biting into the land, a sheer fall to the sea below, guarding one boundary of the meadows ; and the other boundary disappeared into boulders, brambles, gorse and, in summer, a forest of bracken. Below were the rocks, granite and blue elvan pitted with fissures, huge ungainly shapes each part of the whole which sloped without plan inevitably to the sea. Here the seaweed, draped like an apron, thickened the water at low tide ; and gulls, oyster catchers, and turnstones poked among it, uttering wild cries. There was the sense of loneliness, and yet of greatness. This was unmanageable nature, the freedom man chases.

And to us the cliff reflected our endeavour since we came to Minack. It was a part of ourselves. We had seen it those years ago when it was untamed, and visioned the meadows we would carve from the undergrowth, the rich crops we would grow, the sure future we would build. Here we had been a part of some victories and many defeats. We had seen harvests of early potatoes lashed by a gale and destroyed in a night. We had laboured on hot summer days on this cliff shovelling with the long handled Cornish spade beneath the potato plants, Jeannie on hands and knees picking up the potatoes and filling the sacks, then the long steep climb to the top, a sack at a time, journey after journey.

We had rejoiced in the flower season at the sight of the daffodils, dazzling yellow against the blue sea, gulls high above, gannets plummeting offshore ; then gladly endured the steady task of picking, gathering an armful and slowly filling a basket ; and the climb again, heavy basket in either hand. Such as this was our victory. Here in remoteness, a sense of communion with the base of beauty. Not victory in a worldly sense. We produced. We were two of the losing originals. When our efforts left our environment, so did our control. Far away people, cool in their calculations, undisturbed by our hopes, beset with their own problems, decreed our reward.

We had our shield. Moments like the quiet of a Christmas morning when Jeannie and I were together, with a cat called Lama who was born within the sound of the sea.

ACKNOWLEDGEMENTS

" The Claw of Cornwall " is an extract from the book " Vanishing Cornwall " by Dame Daphne du Maurier ; " One Foot in Either County " consists of sections from " Where I Live " by Ronald Duncan ; and " Minack " by Derek Tangye, though newly constructed, are from his books : " Gull On The Roof," " Cat In The Window," " Drake At The Door," " Donkey In The Meadow," " The Way To Minack," and " A Cornish Summer," all published by Michael Joseph.

The remaining 8 chapters are entirely original writings.

BOTH SIDES OF TAMAR
Devon & Cornwall portrayed in words and pictures. 24 illustrations. Price 50p.
Chapters by John Betjeman, Charles Causley, J.C.Trewin, Clive Gunnell, Tom
Salmon, E.W. Martin, Bill Best Harris, James Turner, Jane Toplis and Arthur
Caddick.
". . . a memorable book on Devon and Cornwall."   Western Morning News

". . . a dazzling array of talent."   Arthur Venning, Editor, Cornish & Devon Post

MAKING POLDARK
by Robin Ellis. Over 60 photographs. Price 75p.
The inside story of the popular BBC TV series.
". . . an interesting insight into the making of the TV series . . ."
Camborne Redruth Packet
"It is a 'proper job', as they say, and a credit to all concerned."
Archer in Cornwall Courier

FOLLOWING THE RIVER FOWEY
by Sarah Foot. 49 photographs. Price 90p.
Sarah Foot follows the Fowey from its beginnings on Bodmin Moor to where it
meets the sea beyond Fowey and Polruan.
"She stitches into the simple tapestry of the river's story names and incidents and
anecdotes, deftly and lovingly, every thread and every page touched with charm
and an unashamed sense of delight."   Western Morning News

ALONG THE CAMEL
by Brenda Duxbury and Michael Williams. 60p.
"It is well written, attractively presented, full of historical facts . . ."
"Worth a place on anyone's bookshelf."   Western Evening Herald

THE LIZARD
by Jill Newton.
". . . captures so well the magical atmosphere of the place, full of legend, restless
green seas, crying curlews and sheltered byways . . . deserves a place on the shelf
of any serious collector of Cornish books."
Pamela Leeds, The Western Evening Herald

ABOUT THE CITY
by David Mudd. 44 photographs. Price 90p.
David Mudd takes a look at Truro, telling of ancient charters, the Civil War, of
rivalry with Falmouth, of law and order, fun fairs and funerals, of pills, policemen
and stage coaches. There are even fleeting glimpses of pirates and smugglers.

TINTAGEL TO BOSCASTLE
by Michael Williams. Price 75p.
An illustrated history and guide containing 13 splendid photographs of the region.
". . . one man's view of an enchanting corner of North Cornwall."
Judy McGuire, The Independent

PENZANCE TO LAND'S END
by Michael Williams and John Chard. 40 photographs. Price 75p.
A journey in words and pictures — brilliant photography by John Chard — incor-
porating Newlyn, Mousehole, Lamorna and Porthcurno.

DOWN ALONG CAMBORNE AND REDRUTH

by David Mudd. 44 illustrations. Price 95p.

"spicey but informative . . . extremely good value."

Robert Jobson, Camborne-Redruth Packet

"his journalist's eyes and ears and his sympathy . . . add to the reader's understanding . . ."

West Briton

THE FALMOUTH PACKETS

by David Mudd. 25 illustrations. Price 75p.

". . . the only history of the Falmouth Packet ships to be written in this century . . . vivid and lively . . ."

Enid Thompson, Western Morning News

"An exciting story, lovingly told . . ."

The Falmouth Packet

ABOUT MEVAGISSEY

by Brenda Duxbury. Over 40 illustrations and maps. Price 75p.

". . . an honest, detailed little study which doesn't just tell of a place but brings it gently and evocatively to life."

Western Morning News

"For lovers of Cornwall, About Mevagissey is a must."

Sunday Independent

ALONG THE BUDE CANAL

by Joan Rendell, 49 photographs and map. Price 75p.

The Bude Canal is — or was — a vanishing piece of Cornish history. However, now, thanks to the brilliant researching of Joan Rendell and her ability to get Cornish folk — related to the Canal — to talk, she resurrects it all. Through her words and pictures, we can see it flowing and working once again.

ABOUT LOOE

by Austin Toms and Brenda Duxbury. 38 illustrations. Price 75p.

Austin Toms, a member of the well-known Looe family, talks about old Looe while Brenda Duxbury explores Looe and district today.

"a fascinating collection of memories."

Cornish Times

". . . A double-sided portrait of this double-sided town . . . draws together history, present and future of East and West Looe in one long-overdue volume."

Cornish Life

MY DARTMOOR

by Clive Gunnell of Westward TV — television's most famous walker. Price 95p.

Map and 12 pages of photographs and drawings of Dartmoor wildlife by Robin Armstrong. Introduction by Jeremy Thorpe.

"The work is that of a merry man, and an observant, though kindly one."

Western Morning News

DARTMOOR PRISON

by Rufus Endle. 35 photographs. Price 90p.

"the bleak Devon cage's 170 year history . . . fascinatingly sketched by one of the Westcountry's best known journalists Rufus Endle . . . the man with the key to Dartmoor."

The Western Daily Press

". . . a rare photographic peep into the interior . . . and a fascinating insight into its life and history . . ."

Jean Kenzie, Tavistock Gazette

THE BARBICAN

by Elizabeth Gunnell, 32 photographs. Price 75p.

"Anyone with a love for old Plymouth and the waterfront should not miss this lovely little book. It is outstanding value and highly recommended."

Tavistock Gazette